On the River with
LEWIS AND CLARK

VERNE HUSER

TEXAS A&M UNIVERSITY PRESS

COLLEGE STATION

Library of Congress Cataloging in Publication Data

Huser, Verne.
  On the river with Lewis and Clark / Verne Huser. — 1st ed.
      p.   cm. — (Environmental history series ; no. 19)
  Includes bibliographical references and index.
    ISBN 1-58544-320-4 (cloth, alk. paper); ISBN 1-58544-344-1 (pbk.)
    1. Lewis and Clark Expedition (1804–1806) 2. West (U.S.)—Description
and travel. 3. West (U.S.)—Discovery and exploration. 4. River life —West
(U.S.)—History—19th century. 5. Rivers—West (U.S.)—History—19th
century. 6. Inland navigation—West (U.S.)—History—19th century.
7. Frontier and pioneer life—West (U.S.) I. Title. II. Series.
F592.7 .H87 2003
917.804'2'091693—dc22

                                                        2003015224

All photographs are by Verne Huser unless otherwise noted.

Map and sketches by Heidi H. Hackler, Dolphin Design.

On the River with
LEWIS AND CLARK

NUMBER NINETEEN:
ENVIRONMENTAL HISTORY SERIES
DAN L. FLORES, GENERAL EDITOR

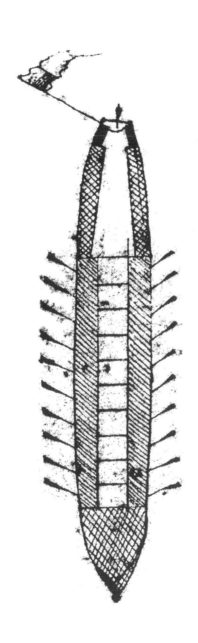

Contents

Preface

As a professional river guide for more than forty-five years, I have long been fascinated by the Lewis and Clark expedition, essentially a river trip. Over the decades I have canoed the lower Columbia, the Jefferson, and the Beaverhead, the middle Missouri border between Nebraska and South Dakota and the upper Missouri in Montana. I have even canoed the Lewis River in Yellowstone National Park, the only segment of the Snake River that retains the Lewis name expedition members gave it, and the Lewis and Clark River on which expedition members built Fort Clatsop.

I have rafted the Madison, the Gallatin, and the Yellowstone and guided raft trips on the Snake in Hells Canyon including the Wild Goose Rapid, visited by members of the expedition in search of spring-run steelhead. With historian Roderick Nash I have cruised up the Columbia from the mouth of the Washougal, where Lewis and Clark camped for several days, to the mouth of the Snake in Nash's Nordic tugboat *Forevergreen*, negotiating the locks in four dams that now block the Columbia, and anchoring at or near several Lewis and Clark campsites.

I have served as Lewis and Clark historian and naturalist for Lindblad Expeditions' cruises on the Columbia and Snake Rivers and for ROW, Inc. commercial canoe trips on the upper Missouri. I have explored the expedition's route through a dozen states (they traveled through areas that have become seventeen states) and led an eighteen-day Elderhostel bus trip along the expedition's route. I have presented conference papers on the Lewis and Clark expedition at Pennsylvania State University and the University of Montana.

A commercial canoe party camps on the upper Missouri.

At the time of Lewis and Clark, rivers were main highways; they provided the medium of transportation and commerce for native people and
Europeans throughout North America. Much of the exploration of the
continent was accomplished by river: Champlain on the St. Lawrence;
La Salle, Marquette, and Joliet on the Mississippi; the Vérendryes on
the upper Missouri; and Hearne, Mackenzie, Thompson, and Simpson
in Canada.

Rivers fascinated Thomas Jefferson. When he planned the initial exploration of the newly acquired Louisiana Territory and well beyond its
nebulous boundaries, he envisioned a river trip across most of the continent: from Pittsburgh, where the keelboat was built, down the Ohio to
the Mississippi, up that core river to the mouth of the Missouri, then up
the Missouri to its headwaters, and over a "pyramidal height of land," the
Continental Divide, and then on to the Pacific by river.

Jefferson knew little about what lay beyond those headwater streams
along the Great Divide. When they started, Lewis and Clark knew little
more than Jefferson did, but they added to their knowledge each day they
traveled, gaining useful information from native peoples and from traders

The official headwaters of the Missouri River lie at the confluence
of the Jefferson and Madison forks, named by Lewis and Clark.
The third fork, the Gallatin, enters half a mile downstream.

and trappers along their route. They all expected to find a river flowing
west toward the Pacific. And so they did, the Columbia, although the short
easy passage over the Divide that they had anticipated did not exist: there
was no Northwest Passage and there was no easy all-water route.

Jefferson instructed Lewis "to explore the Missouri river, & such principal streams of it, as, by it's [sic] course and communication with the
waters of the Pacific ocean, whether the Columbia, Oregon, [sic] Colorado
or any other river may offer the most direct & practicable water communication across this continent for the purpose of commerce."[1]

Water flowing from the Continental Divide toward distant seas on both
sides of the divide served as the party's main medium of travel. The members of the expedition negotiated the waters of three major river systems:
the Ohio, the Missouri, and the Columbia. When you calculate the expedition's total mileage, including three different return routes, they traveled 10,624 miles, 9,046 miles of it by river (5,498 miles downstream, 3,548
miles upstream) during a period of more than three years (August 31, 1803,
through September 23, 1806).

They traveled more than a thousand miles down the Ohio River, 184 miles up the Mississippi, and then 3,096 miles up the Missouri and its tributaries. They named its three forks: the Gallatin, the Madison, and the Jefferson. They followed the Jefferson Fork to the Beaverhead, then the Beaverhead to its founding forks, Horse Prairie Creek and Red Rock River, where the Shoshone Indians met them with horses to help them cross the Continental Divide. Clark explored the Salmon River but found it too full of rapids for safe navigation.

West of the Divide they paddled 640 miles down the Clearwater, Snake, and Columbia Rivers in dugout canoes. The following spring they boated more than two hundred miles up the Columbia through The Dalles to Celilo Falls, where the river began to overpower them. Using horses acquired from local Indians, they traveled overland to the Clearwater, across the Bitterroot Mountains to Traveler's Rest, where Lolo Creek pours into the Bitterroot River, which they called Clark's River. It flows into the Clark Fork, which flows into the Pend Oreille, a Columbia tributary.

Here they split into two groups (ultimately, into five separate parties), each traveling a different route, exploring different ground. Lewis led a third of the party overland to the Great Falls, and then took three men on horseback to explore the headwaters of the Marias River. Clark led the others back to the Missouri's Three Forks and sent Sergeant Ordway with a third of the men down the Missouri to the Great Falls to portage the canoes with the men Lewis had left there. Then Clark led the final third overland to the Yellowstone, where the party built two more canoes and traveled down that significant river to the Missouri.

The Lewis and Clark expedition was more river trip than anything else. In the Foreword to his monumental collection of letters and documents related to the expedition, Donald Jackson wrote, "No one should attempt to understand the expedition from a study of this compilation alone; it is complementary to the journals."[2] Similarly, I write this book as a complement to the journals. Knowledge of the rivers, of their basic functions and common characteristics, and of the most fundamental means of negotiating them should help all readers of the journals to better understanding the Lewis and Clark expedition.

In this book I intend to show how rivers figured in every aspect of the journey from food gathering and fire building to meeting native people and employing basic transportation. I will explore their reasons for traveling by river, the benefits and hazards of river travel.

West of the Continental Divide on the Snake and Columbia Rivers,
the expedition ran into black basaltic rock that created serious rapids.

Then I will describe the boats they used and their means of powering
and maneuvering them. I will also follow their routes both on the rivers
and overland, discussing the river challenges they met and their means
of overcoming them. Finally, I will catalog their accomplishments.

Despite their failure to find a northwest passage and to pacify the native inhabitants, they achieved remarkable success in several disparate
arenas from survival skills and continental exploration to natural history
and ethnology. They were agents of change. Not only did they help open
the American West to further European influence and inspire settlement,
they also altered life styles and cultures of indigenous peoples living along
their route and well beyond the reach of the rivers they followed.

Many natural patterns have been interrupted by human activity since
Lewis and Clark traveled by river across the continent. Patterns that
Lewis and Clark knew have been altered by humankind's obsession with
development, agribusiness, and the internal combustion engine. The
floodplain of the Platte River, which the Corps of Discovery found too
shallow to negotiate, has ironically become a major route for railroads and
highways. As we have turned our collective backs on rivers, using their
floodplains for modern transportation corridors and building sites and
their waters for absorbing wastes and watering crops, we have lost much

of the landscape that so inspired the members of the Lewis and Clark expedition.

In *Taking Care*, William Kittredge, speaking of his father, writes, "He loved the idea of Lewis and Clark, and deeply regretted missing the opportunity to come west when the country was, as he imagined it, stone fresh and prime and new."[3] Bernard De Voto called the Lewis and Clark journals "the most important original narratives of North American exploration"[4] because the story reveals human character at its best and shows us the West in that era. The journals, he wrote, were full of examples of narrow escapes, great hardship, the excitement of discovery, and moments of great exultation. They inspired De Voto.

My own inspiration also came from the expedition journals a half-century ago in the abridged but highly readable De Voto edition (1953), then in the John Bakeless edition (1964). My old friend David Lavender provided me new insights in *The Way to the Western Sea* (1988), and more recently, Stephen Ambrose's *Undaunted Courage* has kept me on course. Then I read the entire Moulton edition of the journals.

I thank Gary Moulton, University of Nebraska history professor, and the University of Nebraska Press for making all the journals available to the public. Moulton's thirteen-volume *The Journals of the Lewis and Clark Expedition*, source of all my journal quotations, is sound scholarship and thorough research. I have retained original spelling and punctuation as it appears in the Gary Moulton edition.

I thank Susan Williamson, librarian at the Albert G. and Barbara Simms Library at the Albuquerque Academy, and the entire library staff, for acquiring the complete set of the Moulton edition that facilitated my research. Dr. James P. Ronda, history professor at the University of Tulsa, has encouraged my efforts; I appreciate his research into the meanings of the expedition as presented in his numerous publications.

Doug Erickson and Jeremy Skinner of the Lewis and Clark College library special collection on the expedition were both helpful in my research efforts as were the libraries at the University of Texas-Austin (my alma mater) and the University of New Mexico, and the staff at the Lewis and Clark Interpretative Center in Great Falls, Montana.

I must also mention practical help from master boat builder Butch Bouvier of Onawa, Iowa, for his counsel concerning the crafts used by the expedition. Beverly Hinds of Sioux Falls, South Dakota, widow of Strode Hinds, a past president of the Lewis & Clark Trail Heritage Foundation, Inc., and a board member at large, was helpful in my research of expedition crafts. The Lewis and Clark Trail Heritage Foundation, Inc., is the primary organization that keeps the expedition's memory alive. (Lewis and Clark Trail Heritage Foundation, Inc., P.O. Box 3434, Great Falls, Montana 59403, 888-701-3434, 406-454-1234, fax 406-771-9237, www.lewisandclark.org.)

I found Paul Russell Cutright's books about the expedition both readable and valuable. Donald Jackson's *Letters of the Lewis and Clark Expedition with Related Documents, 1783–1854* has been especially useful, and Ernest Staples Osgood's *The Field Notes of Captain William Clark, 1803–1805* was a godsend (he knew about thole pins).

Leland D. Baldwin's *The Keelboat Age on Western Waters* was an important source as was Richard C. Boss's article in the *Nautical Research Journal* (June, 1993), "Keelboat, Pirogue, and Canoe: Vessels Used by the Lewis and Clark Corps of Discovery." Boss's son Dick (Richard Jr.), a Forest Service naturalist at the Lewis and Clark Interpretative Center in Great Falls, supplied me with additional papers by his father on the subject. Bob Chenoweth, Curator at the Nez Perce National Historic Park, offered helpful insights about the canoes used by the expedition west of the Continental Divide, as did National Park Service staff at Fort Clatsop National Memorial.

I owe thanks to paddling partners who have explored various river segments with me: David Green, Rod Nash, Jack Remington, Alan Weltzien, Andrew Wingfield, and my son Paul Huser; to Nash for the trip up the Columbia on his Nordic tugboat; to ROW, Inc. for the opportunity to serve as historian on their commercial canoeing trips on the upper Missouri and to Lindblad Expeditions for the privilege of playing a similar role on Lewis and Clark cruises on the Columbia and Snake; and to Chad Cadwell of Missouri River Expeditions, Inc.

David Cane, Ralph Frese, Oz and Dorothy Hawksley, Heidi Hackler (my map-maker, computer consultant, and daughter), Tom Mork, James and Elizabeth Runyan, and Joel Vance all helped, as did my sister Louise Bergman of Des Moines, Iowa, who made my Lewis and Clark era costumes for the various presentations I have made.

I would like to thank my editors Shannon Davies and Dawn Hall for their counsel, direction, and encouragement during the book's evolution. Thanks also go to Barbara Spivey for creating an excellent index.

While the journals are my primary source, I have engaged in some speculation based on my own knowledge of rivers and river navigation. Many aspects of the expedition's river travel were so standard for the period that the journalists fail to address them. I have taken the liberty of attempting to explain them through my personal knowledge and research.

I dedicate this book to my wife, Willa Runyon Huser, who has learned more about the Lewis and Clark expedition than she ever knew she could; who has endured my absence during research in the field and in various libraries; and who has encouraged me all along the way.

On the River with
LEWIS AND CLARK

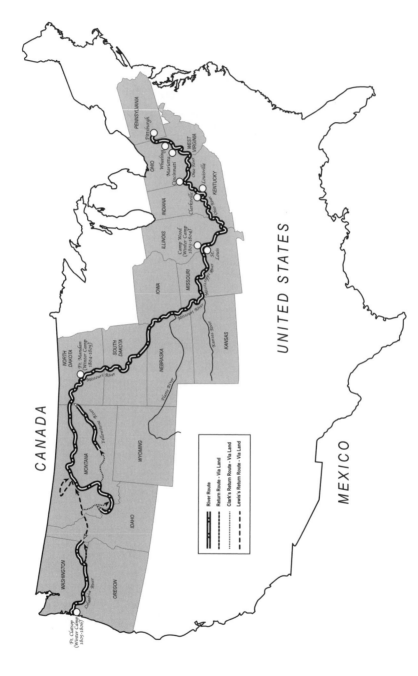

Route of the Lewis and Clark Expedition, by Heidi H. Hackler, Dolphin Design.

Chapter 1

THE WAYS OF WIND AND WATER

On Saturday, April 13, 1805, as the Lewis and Clark expedition moved up the Missouri River above the mouth of the Little Missouri, six days after leaving their winter camp near the Mandan villages, Lewis recorded the day's events: "the wind was in our favour after 9 A.M. and continued favourable untill three 3 P.M. we therefore hoisted both the sails in the White Perogue, consisting of a small squar sail, and spritsail, which carried her at a pretty good gate."[1]

After launching at 6 A.M., according to Clark's journal entry for the day, the party made twenty-three and a half miles against the river's spring snowmelt current, despite an accident that Lewis wrote "was very near costing us dearly," for the white pirogue almost capsized due to a strong sudden gust of wind. Being "the most steady and safe" craft, the white pirogue carried "our instruments, Papers, medicine and the most valuable part of the merchandize which we had still in reserve as presents for the Indians."[2] It also carried three nonswimmers plus Clark's servant York, the Indian woman, Sacagawea, her baby, and the two interpreters, Sacagawea's husband "Sharbono" and George "Drewyer" (Charbonneau and Drouillard).

Lewis described the incident: "about 2 in the afternoon when a suddon squall of wind struck us and turned the perogue so much on the side as to allarm Sharbono who was steering at the time, in this state of alarm he threw the perogue with her side to the wind, when the spritsail gibing was as near overseting the perogue as it was possible to have missed. [that is, without capsizing her] the wind however abating for an instant I ordered

Drewyer to the helm and the sails to be take in, which was instant executed and the perogue being steered before the wind was again plased in
a state of security."[3]

This incident accounted for only about 20 percent of Lewis's journal
entry for the day, but it illustrates the nature of the two natural features
that most affected the voyage, wind and water. Clark mentioned the accident not at all; he spent the day exploring by land, observing "imence
quantity of wild onions or garlick" and "emence numbers of Geese," all
potential food items.

Readers of the Lewis and Clark story will appreciate the accomplishments of the expedition more fully if they know something about the ways
of wind and water, two factors that profoundly impacted the daily lives of
the Corps of Discovery and the ultimate success of the voyage. These natural phenomena greatly affected the expedition's travel plans, thwarting
and frustrating the party at various times, yet also making their expedition
possible and productive.

The physical laws of nature played a vital role in the expedition's progress. Gravity makes water flow downhill. Temperature differential helps
create ocean currents, which affect weather patterns, and wind direction
and velocity. The Coriolis force generated by the spinning of the earth has
a powerful, persistent influence on weather patterns, which affected the
party's progress. Relationships between air pressure and temperature impact weather.

Wind both causes and results from weather patterns. While the expedition used the wind to sail whenever they could, the wind often failed to
blow in a direction favorable to the party's advancement. It frequently
blew in a contrary direction, causing problems and delays. Its sudden gusts
sometimes created especially dangerous situations.

The party's progress can be told in the daily wind patterns it experienced: if the group covered as much as eighteen or twenty miles a day,
traveling upstream against the current, they almost certainly had a tailwind and sailed; if they made fewer then ten miles a day, they quite likely
faced a headwind for several hours. Adverse winds stopped them completely on many occasions. During severe thunderstorms, the wind blew
so suddenly and fiercely that it caused havoc with the boats, creating
waves that filled the crafts, blowing them off the river, capsizing them, or
stopping them dead.

Air masses follow the dictates of gravity, of the Coriolis force, of tem-

A modern explorer uses a downriver wind to negotiate the upper
Missouri by sailing his canoe.

perature differential, even the dictates of the albedo effect (reflected
light). According to canoeist Alan Kesselheim, in *Threading the Currents*,
"If the earth's topography, heat distribution, and surface color were uniform, the atmosphere would lie on us like a quiet cocoon, an unimagined
stillness."[4] But they are not uniform. Kesselheim suggests that the "patch-
work of blue oceans and green forests and white polar regions," help create temperature differentials that cause the winds to blow. Kesselheim
continues, "More than anything else it is the heat of the sun, and the contrast between warm and cool masses of air, that stirs the atmospheric
soup." Wind was both a blessing and a curse to the Lewis and Clark
expedition.

When hot air rises (because it is lighter), cooler, heavier air replaces it.
On a summer day, air over land heats more rapidly than air over water,
creating an upstream airflow that downstream river runners experience
as a headwind. Such upriver winds begin as soon as the day warms, usually mid-morning to early afternoon. Winds follow natural corridors in a
diurnal-nocturnal pattern: unless local storms or larger weather systems in-
terrupt the pattern, the wind blows upstream during the heat of the day
and downstream at night when the land cools.

Traveling down the Ohio River the fall of 1803, Lewis remarked, "the wind on this river . . . blows or sets up against it's courent four days out of five during the course of the whole year," and "the wind so frequently sets up the river the way the traveler makes in descending therefore is by the dint of hard rowing—or force of the oar or pole."[5] Moving the keelboat downstream against the wind required serious work.

River campers who haven't learned about such standard wind patterns will suffer in the smoke of a campfire built in ignorance of the basic diurnal-nocturnal wind-flow system. Experienced boatmen, normally following the river's downstream flow, like to get an early start to avoid battling headwinds later in the day. Aware of this pattern, the Lewis and Clark expedition normally launched at daybreak when there was little or no wind, stopped for breakfast at mid-morning, and then laid over later in the day to avoid the adverse effects of contrary wind.

As powerful a factor as wind became during the expedition's travels, water, a heavier medium, became an even greater issue. Swift currents, low water, serious rapids, and waterfalls all hampered the expedition's progress even as the rivers provided their travel medium and helped them along when they traveled downstream.

Created by nature to drain the land, rivers carve the features of the landscape through which they flow in their varied courses to the ocean. Luna Leopold, one of the world's foremost river geomorphologists, writes in *A View of the River,* that under natural conditions, "The river constructs and maintains its channel."[6] In the process, they carry materials in and on their currents; the stronger the flow, the heavier load they carry.

These materials travel from high mountain headwaters to sea level estuaries, stopping in various forms along the way for hundreds, even thousands of years. Wherever their currents slow, rivers drop their suspended loads in the form of deltas, sandbars, islands, and new river banks. The materials add to the fertility of the river's floodplains and also plant seeds along them. Where moving water slows, especially at the confluence of major rivers in flat terrain, the deposited materials form islands and sandbars.

Rivers erode established banks, cut through bedrock, some of it laid down by ancestral rivers themselves, and carve new channels. Rivers engage in entropy, a general loss of energy, as gravity pulls their waters downstream toward the sea. Rivers flow downhill, from higher elevations to

Lower reaches of the Platte River illustrate the kind of small islands
that mark many river confluences, especially in flat terrain typical
of the Mississippi and lower Missouri Rivers.

lower levels, working all the way to the sea: eroding, depositing, giving
life, and losing energy naturally.

Rivers seek a dynamic equilibrium, a delicate balance between the pull
of gravity and the resistance to flow caused by obstacles in their path,
shorelines, and riverbed. Kesselheim writes, "A river is a dynamic, fussy
power, forever shifting, nibbling at banks, moving rock, laying down silt,
slipping its channel, seeking an elusive equilibrium. A flood only makes
blatant what is usually subtle."[7]

Rivers pick up sediment as they flow, increasing the quantity of sediment and the size of particles they carry as the current increases. When
rivers rise, their velocity increases; their carrying capacity and ability to
move materials along their bottoms increase as well.

When traveling by human-powered craft on a river (the noise of motors
overpowers the natural sounds) it is possible to hear sediments being
thrown against the hull of the craft and rocks rolling along the river bottom. Putting an ear to the tube of an inflatable craft, to the gunnel of a
hard-hulled boat, or to the end of an oar or paddle with its other end in the
water amplifies this aural sensation.

Where the current slows, the suspended particles begin to fall out; first the larger rocks stop rolling, then the smaller ones resist the power of the current and settle. Next, finer gravel precipitates out, followed by sand and silt. Examining an old gravel bar that has been cut through by a recent current reveals layers: large particles at the bottom covered with smaller and smaller sized gravel, then sand, and finally silt.

The Tatshenshini River in British Columbia runs thick and gray with glacial flour—finely ground rock particles that settle when the current slows, flowing across numerous gravel bars. Here the fine silt covers the bars with a veneer of pale mud, which dries and cracks, then turns to powder. Afternoon winds on the Tat lift this powder into the air, creating dust storms nearly every afternoon. Such are the ways of wind and water that the Lewis and Clark expedition experienced: they often ate water-deposited wind-blown sand and silt with their meals.

Rivers constantly change course. Daniel B. Botkin[8] has suggested that Lewis and Clark would hardly recognize the Missouri, even in areas where its flow has not been dammed or diverted, because the river has changed its course so drastically, sometimes moving laterally many miles in the past two hundred years.[9] As Botkin points out, "The river was continually changing its channel, cutting away its banks, depositing sand in new places, and acting in ways that were generally dangerous to the expedition."[10]

Modern dikes and levees restrict rivers, confining them to narrow corridors that actually create floods because the water no longer has access to its natural floodplain. The Army Corps of Engineers' wing dams on the middle and lower Missouri now accelerate the current, deepening the main channel, washing out the meanders, and making river travel more dangerous than it was when Lewis and Clark followed the Missouri.

Since the great Mississippi River floods of 1993, flood-control agencies have finally begun to accept the fact that rivers need room to roam, to move and meander, space to flow into when too much water enters the watershed, whether from severe thunderstorms or sudden and heavy snowmelt. Riparian development and other human activity only exacerbate such flooding.

Dams create calm-water reservoirs that capture sediments, which under normal conditions would settle in floodplains to create natural dikes and provide nutrients to bottomlands. Left alone, rivers create their own dikes: as they overflow their banks, their water spreads; when it spreads, it

Woody debris left by high water litters gravel bars along many free-flowing rivers, creating underwater hazards when high water returns or adding to floating debris in the river.

slows; when it slows, the sediments it has been carrying fall out, leaving a natural fertile levee along the bank. Woody debris brought down by flood-water decorates the riverscape, helps to alter the flow, and creates vital fish habitat.

Confining rivers to narrow corridors to protect floodplain development and farmlands leaves them no place to go but over their banks and onto the land. Rivers rise higher each year, largely because development in the floodplain creates increasingly greater runoff, even as dikes are raised higher. Dikes actually cause additional flooding both upstream and down as floodplains are further restricted. Floods cause even greater devastation when dikes break.

When a dike breaks, water accelerates to such an extent that it erodes unprotected land planted to crops that can't resist the rapid flow. Natural rivers cut broad corridors through their landscapes: witness the Missouri River Valley north of Omaha, Nebraska, between the Loess Hills of Iowa and Blackbird Hill on the Nebraska shore, which Lewis and Clark visited. Human interference usually narrows natural river corridors and leads to flooding.

The middle Missouri flows through a broad valley.

Structural flood control is an expensive and ineffective practice that keeps the Army Corps of Engineers in business and causes more flooding than it prevents. The bed of the Mississippi River in New Orleans is now higher than many of the city's streets; only the dikes keep the rivers from flooding the birthplace of jazz. A well-directed hurricane may someday turn New Orleans into a Venice of the West.

Back to natural rivers, Wendell Berry, in "The Rise," from *The Long-Legged House*, tells of the complex currents that make up a river's flow: "It is not one current, but a braiding together of several, some going at different speeds, some even in different directions."[11] With many currents flowing in several directions at different depths and rates, all rivers, especially powerful ones like the Mississippi, Missouri, and Columbia, cause serious problems for anyone negotiating their surfaces.

Going upstream, the crafts of the Lewis and Clark expedition had to breast the current, which essentially flows downstream. However, wherever the current is deflected or blocked by a barrier—an island, boulder, snag, sweeper, or shoreline protrusion—an eddy is formed, an upstream current created by nature to counteract the downstream flow. Boaters can take advantage of such eddies, but eddies and eddy fences (currents at the edges of eddies) often become hazards or barriers.

Such counter currents were invaluable to the Lewis and Clark expedition as they struggled upstream. (A Mississippi riverboat captain once reported an eddy running for twelve miles upstream at a rate of ten miles an hour.) When they moved upstream, expedition members sought eddies, to use wherever and whenever they found them. Traveling downstream, they avoided eddies and the violent currents at their edges.

Traveling upstream, they stayed as close as possible to the banks, unless the banks were falling in, creating a serious hazard, to take advantage of the slower water near shore, but that practice created other problems: they shattered oars by hitting the bank and once broke their mast on an overhanging branch. The river's current flows stronger on the outside of bends, deepening the channel; the river's depth does not speed the current. In fact, deep water often slows the current.

A boat taking the inside of a bend as a shorter route might go aground because the slower water drops its suspended load of silt, further increasing the shallowness of the shortcut. A river's banks and bottoms create friction that slows the current along the shore and in shallow water.

A rising, accelerating river bows upward in the center, picking up debris, silt, and sand along its edges and bottom. As the expedition headed up the Columbia River the spring of 1806, Private Joseph Whitehouse observed that the rising river carried driftwood. A falling, slowing river tends to trough in the center, depositing silt, sand, and woody debris along the shore and on the bottom. Mark Twain wrote about these typical river patterns decades later, in *Life on the Mississippi*.

Traveling downstream, the expedition boats went with the flow, making better progress, but rapids often blocked that flow. Shallow water, known as shoals, delayed them; falls required portaging baggage and boats around rocky barriers or lining the crafts through swift water. Even traveling with the river's current, the crafts of the expedition reacted to the wind and to the river's eddies and waves.

Kesselheim describes it well: "Current and wind opposing each other raise a strange and unruly conflict on the surface of a river. The current pushes along with its unrelenting force while the winds shove back upstream. The battle piles up steep-sided tricky waves where a canoe tends to twist and tip. The part of the boat in the river is held in the headlong, descending grasp; the hull above water is pushed back, buffeted by the hammering tunnel of air."[12]

The expedition's vessels and the people navigating them drifted with the current before the wind when they could, fought both wind and current when they couldn't, and dealt with both wind and water as necessary to achieve their purposes. They dodged sawyers and sweepers, threaded sandbars and snags, ran rapids and lined chutes, and even used horses and oxen to drag their keelboat (often called "the barge") over shoals on their way down the Ohio. Men were also used as draft animals to tow the heavy cottonwood canoes up the meanders of the Beaverhead. They sailed, rowed and towed, paddled and poled their various crafts: a keelboat, two pirogues, more than twenty different canoes, even skin boats and log rafts. In some cases they simply manhandled the crafts through rapids or carried them around. They learned to play the ocean tides on the lower Columbia.

Even though rivers were highways in the days of Lewis and Clark, they were often undependable. At least two rises occurred annually, the first when local snows began to melt and spring rains refreshed the flow, then again as snow began to melt in the mountains far upstream. Rivers rose with heavy local rains, and they sometimes flooded, but they also ran low in late summer and early fall. They froze during the winter, stopping river traffic.

River levels fluctuate on a daily basis. An especially hot day might be followed by a rise of cold water resulting from snowmelt far upstream. A cool, rainy day might be followed by a drop in river level. Light rain would be absorbed locally, but little snow would melt in the high country because of cooler temperatures. Rivers dwindled with searing summer heat when snowmelt was but a memory. Even the Ohio River ran too low in the late summer of 1803 to float the expedition's keelboat.

In the spring of 1806, when the expedition headed up the Columbia on their return trip from the Pacific, Lewis and Clark found the river flowing some twenty vertical feet higher than it had the previous fall and running much more powerfully. Discouraged by the hard work of powering their heavy canoes up the strong current and manhandling or portaging them through cascades and around falls, they traded for horses, left the river, and proceeded overland. By this time, they had little to haul in the way of trade goods and baggage. When they no longer needed the carrying capacity of the boats, horses served their purpose well.

For several weeks, both on their westward journey and on their homeward return, the expedition members used horses to cross the Continental Divide and the Bitterroot Mountains. They returned to their boats, a single pirogue and several canoes, once they reached the Missouri on their way home. Lewis and Clark each led small parties on horseback to explore other rivers, tributary to the Missouri, before returning to the Missouri and the dash for St. Louis. When they had to haul their cache of faunal and floral materials back to St. Louis and the East, they returned to watercrafts that offered greater carrying capacity.

At last they were going with the flow again, but now the wind became an enemy, blowing upriver so fiercely that at times they had to halt, even lay over to let the wind blow itself out. They avoided what eddies they could, launching at daylight to make as many miles as they could before the upriver winds began.

Water and wind impacted the Lewis and Clark expedition in many ways. The wind certainly helped them sail up the Missouri. It brought weather patterns that both helped and hindered their progress. It even aided their portage of the Great Falls when they raised a sail in a canoe they were hauling by manpower. The wind hindered their advance by blowing from the wrong direction or too hard or too quixotically.

The members of the expedition learned the patterns of the wind to take advantage of the diurnal-nocturnal alterations. At their winter camps, they learned to adjust their chimneys to let the wind keep their cabins clear of smoke. They learned to travel with the wind when it blew in an appropriate direction, to lay over when it didn't, or to try to outsmart it when it blew against them by traveling early or late.

Members of the expedition had to master these two aspects of the natural environment—wind and water. Rain and snow, frost and ice in the river certainly impacted the expedition members with miserable conditions and frostbite, "disagreeable" weather, as several journal keepers called it, but wind and water dominated the elements that caused the expedition some of its most difficult and dangerous incidents yet enabled the expedition to achieve its basic goals.

Chapter 2

THE TRAVELERS

The expedition that President Thomas Jefferson sent west across the continent in 1803 under the command of Meriwether Lewis and William Clark consisted of roughly fifty men. The exact number is impossible to determine from the journals and other historical evidence, but Charles G. Clarke, an expert on the subject, lists fifty-one.[1] Gary Moulton, in Appendix A of volume 2 of the journals, lists forty-nine, including twelve engagés, though it is likely there were no more than eight or nine at any one time. The roster fluctuated.

MERIWETHER LEWIS. President Thomas Jefferson selected his personal secretary to lead the expedition and educated him to the task. Trained in making astronomical observations, Lewis also took crash courses in science, including natural history, and in medical theory and practice. A Virginian who had lived in Georgia as a boy, Lewis joined the army at the age of twenty. Assigned to the Ohio Valley and the Old Northwest Territory, Lewis had served briefly under Captain William Clark. They had become good friends. Better educated than Clark, he wrote extensively, often brilliantly, but there are major gaps in his journals: either he failed to write regularly or many of his notes have been lost.

WILLIAM CLARK. Born in Virginia, the younger brother of Revolutionary War hero George Rogers Clark, William Clark joined the army in 1792, fought in the Old Northwest Territory, and retired at the rank of captain.

A bronze statue of Lewis
and Clark, with Sacagawea
and Pompey below, graces
the waterfront at Fort
Benton, Montana.

Although he outranked Lewis in the regular army and was given the lower rank of second lieutenant for the expedition, Lewis and the men considered Clark co-commander of the expedition and referred to him as Captain. He became the expedition's mapmaker. A better boatman than Lewis, he handled the river activities: hiring boatmen, refitting various crafts, loading the boats, building canoes, facilitating portages.

Jefferson had planned for a small party, no more than twelve to fifteen men. At the Harper's Ferry Armory, Lewis requisitioned only fifteen rifles for the expedition, along with fifteen knapsacks and fifteen overcoats. The supplies and equipment he initially ordered for the expedition reflect the needs of a much smaller party than he eventually recruited.

The permanent party of roughly thirty men included soldiers; three half-Indian interpreters, two of whom were experienced boatmen; a black

Seaman, a huge
Newfoundland dog like
this one, purchased for
twenty dollars in
Pittsburgh, accompanied
the expedition. Seaman
earned his keep by
hunting and serving as
sentry. Photo courtesy
of Aaron Pruzan.

slave; and a Newfoundland dog. As the expedition headed up the Missouri River in the spring of 1804, at least fourteen other men, six soldiers and eight French voyageurs, joined them to man three boats carrying gear and food. Along the way the captains added local interpreters and guides.

A keelboat built in Pittsburgh and three pirogues purchased along the Ohio River served the expedition to transport men, supplies, and equipment down the Ohio River during the late summer and fall of 1803. In November, 1803, when Lewis and Clark headed the keelboat and pirogues up the Mississippi from the mouth of the Ohio, traveling for the first time upstream against a powerful current, they realized that their boats were undermanned and decided to double the number of personnel. The captains, especially Clark, worked the numbers throughout their winter at Camp Wood.

As the party grew in size, so did the load the men would have to haul upstream. Several French-Canadian rivermen and a crew of American soldiers were added to man the two pirogues that augmented the keelboat's carrying capacity. The French rivermen would also serve to train the permanent party in river ways. Before heading up the Missouri on the first leg of their long journey, the number of expedition members roughly tripled from the party originally planned.

The expedition settled into winter camp in southwestern Illinois. Because the land west of the Mississippi, including St. Louis, was still Spanish territory, the expedition established its base camp on the east bank near the mouth of a small tributary, Wood River. The winter camp, known as Camp River Dubois, Camp Dubois, or Camp Wood, lay several miles northeast of St. Louis, opposite the mouth of the river the expedition planned to ascend in the spring.

It was at Camp Wood that captains Lewis and Clark gathered and trained the crew that would become the Corps of Discovery. Its numbers fluctuated as individuals joined the upriver party or dropped off the roster. Some members of the party had come down the Ohio with Lewis; many of the soldiers, Clark, and his Negro slave YORK, had joined the expedition at points along the Ohio. Camp Wood became the expedition's base camp the winter of 1803–1804.

Who were these men sent to find a water route to the Pacific? They were tough young men of many talents. Jefferson instructed the captains to select "backwoodsmen, skilled in hunting and outdoor life and used to hardship."[2] The journals report thirty-three members in the permanent party, including York, who was Clark's slave and boyhood companion and a regular member of the expedition who carried a gun, voted on decisions, and became an asset to the party. Clarke describes him: "kinky-haired, jet-black, large sized, and of herculean strength. A wag, a wit and delight of the party."[3] The Indians were fascinated by the huge black man who often put on a show of ferocity. Indian warriors, pledged to fight to the death, blackened themselves with soot; here was a man blackened all over with a paint that would not wash away (several Indians tried to rub off his black exterior).

Lewis and Clark had three sources of recruits: enlisted men in the army stationed in the West, American frontiersmen from the Ohio Valley, and French boatmen who had settled along the heartland rivers of Illinois and Missouri. The recruits included the "nine young men of Kentucky" often mentioned in the journals: NATHANIEL PRYOR, CHARLES FLOYD, WILLIAM BRATTON, JOHN COLTER, JOSEPH and REUBEN FIELD, GEORGE GIBSON, GEORGE SHANNON (the youngest party member), and JOHN SHIELDS (the oldest party member). Both Joseph Whitehouse and Clark's slave York might be added to the list, for they too were from Kentucky, but these nine were Clark's personal enlistees.

Nine Young Men of Kentucky

PRYOR, thirty-one when he joined the expedition, was one of the older men, married, and a sergeant. Good with horses and often in charge of the horse herd, he became a good boatman as well. The captains described him as "a man of character and ability." Following the expedition he became an officer, rising to the rank of captain. The Pryor Mountains, Pryor Creek, and the town of Pryor in southern Montana still honor his name, as does the town of Pryor, Oklahoma, for he later married an Osage woman and lived with her people in Indian Territory. If he kept a journal, as sergeants were ordered to, it has been lost.

FLOYD, perhaps a distant relative of Clark's, and Pryor's cousin, was another sergeant, the only man who died on the journey. The cause of his death was an apparent ruptured appendix, which would have killed him even if the world's best physician had attended him at that time. The expedition members buried him on a hill overlooking the Missouri River near present-day Sioux City, Iowa. A nearby tributary still bears his name. Until a few days before his death, he kept a journal.

BRATTON was one of the expedition blacksmiths and a good hunter, a tall powerful man "of fine intelligence and the strictest morals."[4] He once swam the river to retrieve his gun and some clothes he had left behind. A trusted man, he was with the party sent back to apprehend the deserter Moses Reed, and he worked on Lewis's iron boat. The painful back problem he acquired as a member of the salt crew on the Pacific coast incapacitated him for several weeks; he was cured by an Indian sweat bath during a month spent among the Nez Perce in the spring of 1806.

COLTER may be the best-known member of the expedition besides the captains and the Shoshone woman Sacagawea, for he is commonly credited with discovering the Yellowstone and Jackson Hole country in present-day northwestern Wyoming. The subject of several books, he is best known for running for his life from a group of Blackfeet Indians near the Three Forks of the Missouri.

In 1810, as he traveled by canoe with expedition member JOHN POTTS, a party of Blackfeet attacked, killing Potts and capturing Colter. The Indians stripped Colter naked and gave him a head start before chasing him across an open cactus-covered plain. He outran the Indians to the river, plunged in, and hid under a logjam (some say in a beaver lodge), escaping after nightfall and then traveling naked to the nearest trading post.

Colter became a valued hunter, courier, and riverman; he often had charge of a canoe. He took an early discharge and, with the captains' blessings, left the expedition at the Mandan villages the summer of 1806 to head back upstream as a trapper. He later worked for the fur entrepreneur Manuel Lisa, carrying word of Lisa's new trading post to the Indians. His first-hand knowledge of the upper Missouri became valuable to Clark as he reworked his maps.

JOSEPH and REUBEN FIELD, the only brothers on the expedition, were reliable hunters who furnished meat for the hard-working members of the Corps of Discovery. They were often chosen for reconnaissance duty; both were with Lewis on the Marias when they encountered the Piegan Blackfeet. Reuben Field fatally stabbed a young warrior, the only Indian known to have been killed by an expedition member (Lewis shot another who may have recovered). Lewis wrote of the Field brothers, "It was their peculiar fate to have been engaged in all the most dangerous and difficult scenes of the voyage, in which they uniformly acquited themselves with much honor."[5]

GEORGE GIBSON, a fiddler who knew Indian sign language, was a hunter and horseman who sometimes served as an interpreter. At Camp Wood he won a shooting competition. On July 14, 1804, when high waves almost inundated the keelboat in a storm, a pirogue under his charge fared much better due to his boating skills. He often served as a messenger to the Indians and was with Lewis when the captain first sighted the Great Falls of the Missouri. On the Clearwater, he helped repair a damaged canoe, and with Cruzatte, entertained the Indians.

GEORGE SHANNON, a Pennsylvanian of Irish descent, nearly starved on the voyage up the Missouri the summer of 1804, and earned an undeserved reputation for getting lost. Thinking that the expedition had passed him on the river while he was hunting, he headed upstream on horseback, but the party was behind him and couldn't make as many miles on the river as he did on land. Having run out of lead, he once used a wooden stick as a bullet to kill a rabbit, his only food for a week.

In the Beaverhead country the following summer, Shannon was sent up the Big Hole River to hunt before the men learned that they had gone up the wrong fork. Unaware that the expedition had taken the other fork, he was missing for three days but returned safe. A fine horseman, he accompanied Sergeant Pryor with the horse herd and subsequently floated several hundred miles down the Yellowstone and Missouri in a bullboat.

JOHN SHIELDS, a relative of Daniel Boone, was a skilled and creative blacksmith, one of the older men at thirty-five, and one of the few married men. Clarke called him "one of the most valuable men on the expedition, as he was the head blacksmith, gunsmith, boat builder and general repair man for anything needed."[6]

Some authorities add JOSEPH WHITEHOUSE to the nine young men of Kentucky, for he had lived in the state before joining the expedition. An enlisted man who kept a journal, Whitehouse was the party's hide-curer, chief tailor, and moccasin maker. The Whitehouse journal gives more details of the means of river travel than either the captains' journals or any of the sergeants' journals. He also had a quixotic penchant for applying appropriate names to sites, many of which were used by the captains in their writings. He provides much of the humor in the collective journals.

Frontiersmen and Boatmen

SERGEANT JOHN ORDWAY, a native of New Hampshire and the only regular army sergeant, served as a sort of sergeant major. He handled the military paperwork and duty rosters and commanded the party at Camp Wood in the absence of the captains. He was the most consistent journal keeper of the Corps of Discovery. From the Three Forks of the Missouri to the Great Falls, he commanded the boat party that returned from the canoe cache on the Beaverhead. He supervised the eastward portage of the Great Falls and picked up Lewis and his three men following their battle with the Piegan Blackfeet on the Marias headwaters.

A Pennsylvanian of Irish ancestry, PATRICK GASS joined the army at eighteen. Short and broad, he was the best carpenter of the Corps of Discovery. He supervised the building of Fort Mandan and Fort Clatsop where the party wintered and oversaw canoe building. Upon the death of Sergeant Floyd, the men elected Gass to replace him. Gass's journal was the first published (1807); it became a popular book, frequently reprinted. He died a few months shy of ninety-nine (in 1870), the last known survivor of the Corps of Discovery.

At St. Charles two experienced Missouri River boatmen, FRANÇOIS

LABICHE and the one-eyed fiddler PIERRE CRUZATTE, joined the army for the expedition rather then hiring on as *engagés*. Both men had French fathers and Omaha Indian mothers; they spoke both French and Omaha. Labiche also spoke English, and Cruzatte may have known English as well. Both had lived with their mothers' tribe and had traded with other Missouri River Indians. They served as interpreters and as vital members of the keelboat crew and often served on the pirogues as well. Nearsighted in his only good eye, Cruzatte accidentally shot Lewis in the buttocks as the party returned down the Missouri the summer of 1806.

The third half-Indian was GEORGE DROUILLARD (usually DREWYER in the journals), son of a French father and a Shawnee mother, and the subject of the novel *Sign Talker* by James Alexander Thom. On the river, he frequently saved the day, for he was another experienced boatman. A civilian employee gifted in the Plains Indian sign language, he proved to be the party's best hunter, scout, and most reliable interpreter, their most important negotiator with the Indians. Nearly every time Lewis explored overland, Drouillard accompanied him. He was with Lewis and the Field brothers in the fight on the Marias. Like Colter and Potts, after the expedition, he had returned to the upper Missouri as a trapper, working for Manuel Lisa. Drouillard was killed by Blackfeet Indians near the Three Forks of the Missouri in 1810.

Many members of the permanent party, while drawn from a variety of hardy and practical backgrounds, had special talents—or soon developed them. Besides Bratton and Shields, ALEXANDER HAMILTON WILLARD knew the blacksmithing trade. During the winter of 1804–1805, the trio kept the expedition well fed with the Indian corn, beans, and squash they traded for the metal battle-axes that the Mandan craved. Clark later hired Willard as blacksmith for various Indian tribes. A native of New Hampshire, he may have kept a journal, but it has not been found.

The larger (red) seven-oared pirogue was manned by experienced rivermen, largely French-Canadian voyageurs, a close-knit crew who knew what they were doing on the river. These French rivermen were not members of the permanent party nor were they military men. Hired for the specific purpose of hauling a heavy load to the advanced base camp at the Mandan villages, these men were mostly ignored as individuals by the journal writers (none of the journal writers rode the red pirogue), but they were vital to the expedition's success.

They no doubt helped train the American crew in the skills of powering and maneuvering the crafts upriver—by example and shame, challenge and goad. Members of the red pirogue's crew, released from duty after accomplishing their aim, returned down the Missouri that fall, traveled overland to visit relatives in Canada, or wintered with tribes along the upper Missouri, some with the expedition at Fort Mandan.

Engagés

There is some question about the exact number of engagés with the expedition; it varied from time to time. JEAN BAPTISTE DESCHAMPS, the patroon (river boss), was hired for his experience and maturity. Ten other men have been listed as crew members for the red pirogue, but some dropped off the team before the party left Missouri.

E. CANN may have been ALEXANDER CARSON and may have been related to Kit Carson. He wintered with the Arikara in 1809–1810, and then joined the westbound Astorians in 1811, worked for both the North West Company and Hudson's Bay Company (HBC), and eventually settled in the Willamette Valley of Oregon. CHARLES CAUGEE is listed as an engagé on July 4, 1804, but he may have dropped from the expedition early. JOSEPH COLLINS is listed as an engagé on May 26, 1804, but is not mentioned again. CHARLES HEBERT is listed on the May 26, 1804, roster but nowhere else.

ETIENNE MALBOEUF, a Canadian whose mother may have been Indian, lived in Kaskaskia, Illinois, when he joined the expedition as a hired boatman. He returned the spring of 1805, possibly with the keelboat.

JEAN BAPTISTE LA JEUNESSE, a Canadian married to Malboeuf's sister, was discharged at the Mandan villages in the fall of 1804. He headed down the Missouri by canoe on November 6, with Paul Primeau, and may have wintered with one of the tribes along the river.

LA LIBERTÉ (JOSEPH LE BARTE), the infamous deserter, was caught but escaped. A good riverman, he was assigned to the keelboat and to a pirogue at various times. Donald Jackson speculated that he may have been Joseph Collins. In any case, he deserted near the Oto villages; he knew the Oto language and may have joined that tribe.

PETER PINAUT may also be CHARLO, the son of a French father and a Missouri Indian mother. PAUL PRIMEAU left the Mandan villages when the expedition no longer needed his services and headed downriver by canoe the fall of 1805, with Jeunesse, and may have wintered with the Arikara.

FRANÇOIS RIVET was a famous name on the western rivers. He was born in Montreal but moved to the Mississippi Valley at an early age. He became a hunter, riverman, and trader, from Louisiana to the Missouri. After the expedition, he moved to the Flathead country west of the Divide, worked as a trapper and interpreter on the Columbia, and settled in the Willamette Valley of Oregon at the age of seventy-eight, where he died at ninety-five in 1852.

PETER ROI (ROKEY?) may have been born in Missouri, lived with tribes on the upper Missouri, and returned to St. Louis with the expedition in 1806. He was not with the return party in the spring of 1805. He was not with the expedition from the fall of 1804 to the summer of 1806 but may have met them a time or two on their voyage and joined them on their return.

The smaller (white) six-oared pirogue was manned by a crew of American soldiers who knew little about maneuvering and powering pirogues. CORPORAL RICHARD WARFINGTON had charge of the white pirogue when the expedition left Camp Wood in the spring of 1804. It was manned by six private soldiers, five men permanently assigned to the craft, and one assigned from the keelboat each day. A North Carolinian, Warfington performed his duties so well that he was given command of the keelboat for its return trip to St. Louis in the spring of 1805.

Warfington's crew included JOHN BOLEY, JOHN DAME, EBENEZER TUTTLE, ISAAC WHITE, and ROBERT FRAZER. Boley became so good a boatman that he later accompanied Zebulon M. Pike's expeditions to the upper Mississippi (1805) and to the Rockies (1806). He went down the Arkansas River to the Mississippi, then down the Mississippi to New Orleans with Pike's party. (Pike did not go down the Arkansas; Spanish authorities captured him in New Mexico Territory.) Frazer joined the permanent party at Fort Mandan, replacing the deserter Moses Reed.

At the Mandan villages, where the party spent the winter of 1804–1805, the captains hired another French trader, Toussaint Charbonneau, and his teenaged Shoshone wife, Sacagawea, pregnant at the time. The whole family would join the expedition's permanent party.

TOUSSAINT CHARBONNEAU (1758–1842). In spite of his reputation as a cradle robber and wife beater, Charbonneau was a valued interpreter and the expedition's best cook. He served the expedition well even though he lacked the water skills of most of the Frenchmen on the expedition. The

Metal cut-out figures representing Lewis, Clark, and Sacagawea line
the Snake River's west bank below the mouth of the Clearwater
at the northern edge of Clarkston, Washington.

oldest member of the expedition, forty-six when he joined at Fort Mandan the winter of 1804–1805, Charbonneau had lived among the Hidatsa
as an independent trader; he knew the native people and their languages.
Clark liked Charbonneau, and after the expedition often hired him as an
interpreter during his career as Superintendent of Indian Affairs.

SACAGAWEA (1788?–1812). Only a teenager during her expedition involve-
ment, Sacagawea served the expedition as interpreter and peace symbol,
not as a guide. The wife of interpreter Charbonneau, she had been captured by the Hidatsa near the Three Forks of the Missouri about 1800
when she was eleven or twelve. A Lemhi Shoshone, she was the sister of
Cameahwait, the chief whose band the expedition first contacted and
from whom they acquired horses for their overland trip to the Pacific.

*Sacagawea has been credited with being the expedition's guide, a
characterization that is less than accurate. She knew little of the route
the expedition traveled, having been captured as a child and taken*

overland, not by river, to her new home at the Hidatsa village near Fort Mandan. Traveling with the expedition, she recognized the Three Forks area where she had been captured some years earlier, and Beaverhead Rock, namesake of the Beaverhead Fork of the Jefferson River. She knew they were nearing her home country, but she did not guide them up the Missouri; they merely followed the river as Jefferson had ordered them to do.

On the return trip, when Clark led one-third of the party over what is now Bozeman Pass to the Yellowstone River, she may have served as guide, for she had been over that route as a child with her people on the way to the buffalo country for their annual hunt.

Sacagawea's primary role on the expedition was as interpreter for the horse trading with the Shoshone tribe; it was just good luck that the Shoshone band the expedition encountered was led by her brother. Her presence as a woman with a child signaled to every tribe they met that the expedition came in peace. She helped break the ice with several tribes west of the Divide. Then too, as an Indian woman, she knew edible plants and frequently augmented the expedition's diet with foods that not only made meals more palatable but more nutritious.

During the winter at Fort Mandan, JEAN BAPTISTE LEPAGE, another French trapper, enlisted as a permanent party member to replace JOHN NEWMAN, who had been court-martialed for "expressions of a highly criminal and mutinous nature" and expelled from the expedition. During the winter at Fort Mandan, Newman tried to redeem himself with hard work but was sent back to St. Louis with the return party the spring of 1805. Trapping on the middle Missouri in the 1830s, he was killed by Yankton Sioux, a tribe that had been well disposed toward members of the expedition the summer of 1804.

Lepage had lived with the Cheyenne, had been to the Black Hills at the head of the Little Missouri, and probably provided Clark with useful information for his map; he likely did some translating.

In the course of their travels, the captains often hired local Indian guides and interpreters. Some conversations were translated through four or five languages each way; interpreters were essential to the expedition's understanding of and trade with native people, and to its ultimate success in communicating with local tribes.

Statues of the Shoshone Indian woman, Sacagawea, usually depict her pointing, as though she were the expedition's guide. In fact, she served as interpreter and peace symbol. If she ever guided the party, it was along a plain trail over present-day Bozeman Pass.

Other Expedition Members

JOHN COLLINS had drinking problems at Camp Wood. He shot a local farmer's pig and tried to pass it off as bear meat. On the upriver voyage he was court-martialed for stealing whiskey that he was assigned to guard. Yet he became a useful member of the permanent party. A small creek in the Bitterroots was named for him. He served as a cook and hunter. After the expedition, he became a trapper, joined William Ashley on the upper Missouri, and was killed in Ashley's battle with the Arikara (1823).

SILAS GOODRICH, a regular army man and native of Massachusetts, was the best fisherman in the permanent party. He kept the expedition well supplied with fish on both sides of the great Divide: catfish on the lower and middle Missouri, trout on the upper Missouri, and salmon and steelhead on the Clearwater, Snake, and Columbia Rivers.

HUGH HALL and THOMAS PROCTOR HOWARD were both from Massachusetts and both had drinking problems. During the winter at Camp Wood,

Clark wrote of Howard, "he never drinks water." Hall was court-martialed for tapping into the expedition's whiskey supply and getting drunk with Collins. A nonswimmer, he joined Pryor's overland horse party to avoid traveling on the river. Ironically, when the horse herd was stolen, he floated several hundred miles down the Yellowstone and Missouri Rivers in a primitive bullboat. Otherwise, his service was unremarkable.

HUGH MCNEAL, a Pennsylvanian who made the entire journey, was involved in an incident at Fort Clatsop. A local Indian, covetous of McNeal's blanket, planned to kill him, but the plot was discovered and thwarted; Whitehouse called a nearby creek "McNeal's Folly." McNeal had a harrowing encounter with a grizzly bear on the eastward portage of the Great Falls: McNeal clubbed the bear over the head with his rifle, and the bear kept McNeal treed for several hours.

JOHN POTTS, a German miller, was the only expedition member not born in North America. MOSES REED was the lone member of the permanent party to desert. JOHN ROBERTSON (ROBINSON) remains a mystery, a ghost. His name appears on the Orderly Book for April 1, 1804, six weeks before the party left Camp Wood, but is not listed in the detachment order of May 26, 1804, when the men were assigned to squads. JOHN B. THOMPSON seems to have had some surveying background, for he helped Clark with the instruments used to make observations.

PETER M. WEISER (often *Wiser* in the journals), born and raised in Pennsylvania, was second to Reuben Field in a shooting match at Camp Wood, where he had some disciplinary problems but made the cut to become a member of the permanent party. After the expedition he joined Manuel Lisa's fur trade on the upper Missouri and Yellowstone. He may have trapped in the Snake River drainage, for a river and town in western Idaho have his name.

WILLIAM WERNER (often *Warner* in the journals) had disciplinary problems several times; he was appointed cook and was once used as a messenger; and his participation in the expedition is characterized as "satisfactory but unremarkable." RICHARD WINDSOR was a good shot often assigned to hunt.

Taken as a whole, the members of the Lewis and Clark expedition were a hardy lot, a bit wild at times but duty-bound to complete the task for which they had volunteered. They worked diligently, suffered hardships, and nearly starved, but they proceeded on to become famous as they added a vital chapter to early American history.

Chapter 3

THE BENEFITS AND HAZARDS
OF RIVER TRAVEL

The Lewis and Clark expedition traveled across the continent by river because President Thomas Jefferson ordered them to do so. He had sound reasons for his directive. At the time of the expedition, rivers were the established medium for hauling heavy, bulky goods over long distances. Besides, rivers would supply the expedition with drinking water; food in the form of wild game and edible river-bottom plants; and accessible campsites with plenty of firewood and timber for building boats, repairing and replacing masts, poles, oars, and paddles. Rivers also offered access to the native people whose trade Jefferson wanted to capture for American merchants.

Rivers were the highways of late-eighteenth- and early-nineteenth-century America, which is the primary reason most population centers developed on rivers. Even though rivers powered mills, grinding grain and sawing timber, transport was their principal function. If a town or village had no river nearby, its commercial potential was uncertain. The few roads were frequently too muddy for reliable travel, and Indians and thieves ruled the wild lands between settlements. They even threatened river travelers, though rivers offered a certain degree of protection.

To go somewhere that rivers didn't go, people either walked, in which case their load had to be light and they could not travel many miles a day, or they rode horseback, which meant they could carry a bit more baggage and cover more miles, but the horse might go lame or be stolen, and it had to be fed and watered. To haul produce to market, early settlers used wagons drawn by horses or oxen, and it was necessary to travel the precarious roads or make new ones. Living near a river offered access to reliable transportation, and even then seasonal water-level fluctuations and winter ice shut down traffic.

River travel had long been the means of delivering wheat, whiskey, beeswax, honey, iron implements, coal, livestock, and lumber to markets throughout the frontier West along the Allegheny, Monongahela, Ohio, and Mississippi. When Zadok Cramer's famous book, *The Navigator*, first appeared in 1801, it offered advice on every aspect of river travel "with accurate maps of the Ohio and Mississippi." This early river guidebook, updated frequently, was standard fare for anyone heading west by river; Lewis probably had a copy when he left Pittsburgh. The title page of the 1808 edition includes "An account of Louisiana and of the Missouri and Columbia Rivers as discovered by the voyage under captains Lewis and Clark."

Cramer's advice to river travelers: first "procure a boat." He warns against "the unpardonable carelessness and penuriousness of the boat builders" as the cause of most accidents.[1] The best seasons to travel, he suggests, are spring and fall; he advises, "land as seldom as possible" (because landing caused loss of time and involved navigation hazards and vulnerability to thieves). He warns against weak towlines because "the strength of your cable is a great safeguard."[2]

At the time of the Lewis and Clark expedition, even the lower Missouri was becoming well known and heavily used. As it worked its way slowly up the Big Muddy, the expedition met parties of traders and trappers two or three times a week coming down the Missouri in a wide assortment of crafts—bateaux, canoes, mackinaws, pirogues—carrying pelts, buffalo robes, tallow, and dried meat.

The rivers provided water and a steady food supply for the expedition. There were fish in the water, and the riparian habitat provided wild game that sustained the men for most of their journey. Edible roots, wild grapes, cherries, currents, plums, and berries grew on the banks. Such delicacies as watercress grew in the river. Only when they traveled overland, away from the rivers, did the men of the expedition want for food.

Jefferson's primary purpose in sending Lewis and Clark across the continent was to establish a trade route by water. He hoped to open trade with the Indians and to expand American influence to the Pacific. He also wanted to generate peace among the tribes and to lure them away from British influence by bringing them into the fold of American commerce to secure the West for the United States. The native people whom the expedition expected to encounter lived on or near the rivers. As Nez Perce elder Allen Pinkham once told me, "The rivers are the blood vessels of our Mother Earth." The Corps of Discovery followed the rivers through the living heart of the land, a place where people made their homes.

Rivers provided protection from hostile Indians on shore because camping on islands provided a barrier against surprise attack. During their encounter with the Teton Sioux, the expedition anchored offshore overnight and the next day met the Sioux leaders on an island at the mouth of the Bad River. When Lewis and his small party returned from their deadly encounter with the Piegan Blackfeet, they took to the river as soon as possible and after traveling several miles downstream, camped on the opposite shore. With the river at their backs, they usually felt safe camping on shore.

The river offered fast, easier downstream travel. Going with the flow, they made three to six times the mileage as traveling against the current. Their first day down the Beaverhead (June 10, 1806) on their return voyage, they made nearly a hundred miles. Clark's party traveled seventy miles on their first day going down the Yellowstone (July 24, 1806). On the Missouri (August 13, 1806) "by the assistance of the wind, the Current and our oars,"[3] they covered eighty-six miles in one day. Traveling with the current, they made excellent mileage. Both the expedition's goals and its success depended on its traveling by river.

BENEFITS OF RIVER TRAVEL

To Find a Commercial Water Route

As mentioned above, the reason that the Lewis and Clark expedition traveled by river was that Jefferson ordered them to do so. His primary goal in sponsoring the expedition was to find a water route to the Pacific for the purpose of commerce. As James P. Ronda points out, Thomas Jefferson, long obsessed with rivers, saw the Missouri as "the master river for American expansion. It was empire's clear path."[4]

When Lewis wrote that he might make a side trip to Santa Fe over the winter of 1803–1804, Jefferson wrote back to set him straight as to the expedition's purpose: "The object of your mission is singular, the direct water communication from sea to sea formed by the bed of the Missouri and perhaps the Oregon."[5]

Jefferson used the exploration of the Louisiana Territory as a pretext for sending Lewis and Clark to the Pacific by river. He hoped they would discover a Northwest Passage, an easy water route across the continent. The expedition was primarily a scouting party for westward expansion, sponsored by the federal government, using the most common means of transportation for the period.

To Haul Gear and Provisions

The Lewis and Clark expedition may have been the best-provisioned expedition in the history of American exploration, but to haul all the gear and equipment, supplies and provisions, required the carrying capacity offered only by river craft. Although some accounts estimate the expedition's load at a mere thirty-five hundred pounds, most scholars consider that a minimal figure. Richard L. Boss has calculated the carrying capacity of the three crafts that hauled the load up the Missouri at closer to thirty tons: twelve to fourteen tons for the keelboat, nine for the red pirogue, and eight for the white pirogue, a figure verified by Clark's sketch of the craft.

The accurate figure probably lies somewhere between the two, but the fact remains that they had a heavy load to haul a long way. They would have needed more than five hundred horses and mules to haul that load overland. This would have been a tempting pack string for Plains Indians who were notorious horse thieves, as the expedition members learned on several occasions.

To Provide Food and Water

Fish lived in the rivers the expedition traveled: catfish in the lower Missouri, cutthroat trout in its upper tributaries; salmon and steelhead in the Clearwater, Snake, and Columbia; eulachon and sturgeon in the lower Columbia. They even found and ate crayfish in the creeks as they traveled over the Bitterroots. The riparian habitat offered many edible plants as well.

Twice they seined a lake near the river and caught hundreds of fish. Silas Goodrich, an excellent fisherman, kept the party well supplied with piscatorial pleasures and delightful diversions from their steady meat diet

Oregon grape, which Lewis described at the Cascades of the
Columbia on April 11, 1806, is among the edible plants including
roots, fruits, nuts, and berries that the expedition found along the
river corridors. Its flower, seen here, produces an edible fruit.

of deer, elk, bear, buffalo, beaver, pronghorn, bighorn sheep, ducks, geese,
cranes, swan, grouse, and other birds, all of which they found in abundance along the rivers. Most of their hunting and meat gathering at Fort
Clatsop they did by canoe on the river.

Wild game served as their main food. On July 13, Lewis wrote, "We eat
an emensity of meat; it requires 4 deer, an Elk and a deer, or one buffaloe,
to supply us plentifully 24 hours."[6] Lewis suggested at one point that they
killed only what they needed, but before long as the party found bounti-
ful wildlife, they began killing much more game than they could possibly
have used.

Traveling up the Missouri, they entered a region of plentiful pronghorn. Near the Gates of the Mountains they found abundant bighorn
sheep. Bear meat was part of their regular diet throughout the expedition;
oil rendered from bear fat was a dietary staple. Buffalo remained a favorite
food, especially boudins (sausage, "a delicacy made from buffalo intes-
tine"[7]) as Charbonneau prepared them. Remember, he was one of the best
cooks on the expedition.

The men trapped beaver for their pelts, but they ate their meat as well.

Elk, almost always with a capital E in the journals, were an
important food source for the expedition. Lewis wrote that feeding
the expedition required four deer or a deer and an elk or one buffalo
daily. Each man ate several pounds of meat every day.

They considered beaver tails a delicacy, and the rich dark meat tasted like
pork. Several expedition members were experienced trappers; after the
expedition a handful became professional trappers on the Missouri and
Yellowstone. They helped supply Clark with information that enabled
him to expand the territory covered by his map.

Whenever the expedition members found a new species of mammal or
bird, they ate it—everything from prairie dogs to raven. They ate the meat
and blubber of a whale found on a Pacific beach near the mouth of the Columbia. In the mountains they found grouse; on the Snake River Plain
they found and ate sage grouse. They even ate coyotes and wolves.

Near the mouth of the Columbia they often dined on waterfowl: several varieties of ducks and geese, herons, cranes, and swans. Today the islands on the lower Columbia a few miles above Astoria, Oregon, abound
in waterfowl as I discovered in April, 2002, while canoeing through the
Lewis and Clark National Wildlife Refuge. We saw mallards, pintails, and
teal as well as Canada geese and great blue herons, but no swans.

Not all creatures that live on the river are considered edible, fishy mer-
gansers and cormorants, for example, but the men of the expedition tried

most of them. Even creatures that lived on the plains, with the possible exception of the prairie dog, depended on river water and sooner or later appeared along the riverbank to drink.

Water was always available to expedition members when they traveled by river or along streams, which provided the easiest overland routes. The river water was sometimes muddy and often repulsive, especially below a buffalo crossing or when they found dozens of dead buffalo floating in it. But it did quench their thirst and keep them hydrated. On the lower Columbia where tidal ocean waters mix with fresh water flowing down the mighty river, they had to collect rainwater or take their drinking water from small freshwater tributaries, but essentially the rivers they traveled provided them with drinking water.

To Provide Building Material and Fuel

The canoes built on five different occasions they carved from trees that grew along the river or near it. The cottonwood dugouts made at Fort Mandan they hewed from trees found more than a mile from the river but obviously within the river's floodplain. Even the iron-framed skin boat that failed them required wood to brace the frame and hold it in place. The expedition members usually found wood along the river, either growing there or carried down from upstream as driftwood.

As noted, riverside timber supplied wood for masts, spars, poles, oars, and paddles, which kept breaking or wearing out or being lost to the river. A few days into their journey, sailing too close to shore in order to take advantage of the bankside eddy, the keelboat's mast broke on an overhanging sycamore limb and had to be replaced. Once, the men found abandoned tipi poles that served well as setting poles.

Even on the portage of the heavy dugout canoes around the Great Falls of the Missouri, the men used local timber for their wagon wheels, sawing boles from a twenty-two-inch-diameter cottonwood tree. For portaging canoes around the cascades and falls of the Columbia they used log rollers, found as driftwood on the riverbank. Without riverside timber, the expedition would have had a tough time completing its journey.

Normally, but by no means always, the river supplied firewood to cook the men's food, dry their meat, warm their bodies, and keep the mosquitoes at bay. Even in areas where little timber grew, driftwood and beaver cuts from upstream sources collected in high water eddies and on the points of islands and could be gathered. However, firewood became scarce in areas where concentrated populations of indigenous people lived. The Corps sometimes had to purchase or trade for firewood to do their cooking.

To Provide Protection

The expedition often camped on islands as a precaution against man and beast, but islands weren't always the safest campsites. Once, in the middle of the night, the river washed away the island on which they were camped; they had to take to the boats in a hurry to avoid being swept away. The expedition used the moving water as a barrier, but it sometimes turned against them.

To Provide Transportation

Rivers provided the expedition with its major medium of transportation for 85 percent (9,046 of 10,624 miles) of its journey. The captains frequently referred to the expedition as a voyage. They went where the rivers took them, but they knew, in general, where they needed to go.

Even frozen rivers served them well. During their winter at Fort Mandan, ice bridges across the frozen Missouri provided the men access to Indian villages on the opposite shore where they gathered information about what lay ahead farther up the Missouri and along the Continental Divide. Frozen rivers also expanded their hunting territory.

The expedition was a river trip, not the first in North America by any means, but one of the longest ever attempted. The continent was explored and colonized by river. Fort Benton on the upper Missouri was a major center for the settling of Montana as late as the 1880s. The Corps of Discovery showed these settlers and others the way. For nearly a century the rivers led humanity into the interior: first the mountain men, then the settlers, finally the entrepreneurs of commerce and industry. Steamboats, then the railroads, followed the river, and finally the roads and highways.

HAZARDS OF RIVER TRAVEL

For all the advantages of traveling by river, hazards still exist. By definition, a hazard is a risk, a peril, a danger; jeopardy, an obstacle. Members of the Lewis and Clark expedition knew them all. They took risks and found themselves in perilous situations; they faced danger, often several times a day. They lived in almost constant jeopardy from such natural elements as weather, wildlife, fire, and flood. Their strenuous work added another dimension to the hazards they faced. Yet they survived and surmounted the numerous obstacles they encountered, both on and off the river, over a period of more than three years.

Isolation was neither the least of their problems nor the most obvious, but it played a significant role during the expedition. Besieged by beasts, worried by weather, haunted by hunger, sullied by sickness, expedition members threaded their way through hostile indigenous tribes across what seemed an unknown wilderness. Although it was well peopled and much of it relatively well known, at least as far as the Mandan villages where the Corps of Discovery spent the winter of 1804–1805, the Louisiana Territory separated the men from their own kind.

River hazards added to the expedition's natural risks and perils. A common axiom among river runners says that most accidents on river trips happen off the river. However true this may be, the very fact that the expedition traveled primarily by river led them into infinite dangers, directly or indirectly related to river travel.

Drowning claimed many lives among early-day rivermen. Several members of the expedition could not swim; they wore no life jackets and they did not have the throw-ropes that modern river runners use to rescue a "swimmer" (anyone in the river as a result of falling out of a boat, swamping, or capsizing). Interpreter Toussaint Charbonneau, a notorious nonswimmer terrified of the river, nearly brought the expedition to grief on two different occasions through his fear of water.

Rivers are not inherently dangerous, certainly not treacherous, as modern reports of floods and river accidents suggest. Rivers were no more treacherous during the early nineteenth century than they are today; they are simply indifferent to the human world. They follow basic immutable natural laws that govern fluvial flow; those who fail to recognize or respond appropriately to these laws are likely to suffer the consequences.

The men often worked in the water, manhandling the boats over shoals or towing them through rapids or fast water, sustaining injuries when caught between a swamped canoe and an underwater rock or log. Such accidents crushed the legs of Howard, Thompson, and Whitehouse. Colter's horse tumbled with him down a creekbed in the Bitterroots. Bratton's bad back incapacitated him for months; Sergeant Pryor frequently dislocated his shoulder; others wrenched knees and sprained ankles. A snake bit one man.

Everyone had torn, bruised, and battered feet from towing in shallow water full of slick, mossy river boulders or along shores lined with sharp unstable rocks, thorny vegetation, and beaver cuts. Traveling overland, even Lewis's dog, Seaman, suffered from prickly pear thorns in its paws; all the men, including the captains, suffered from thorns in their feet.

Several times men had to leap out of boats into the river to prevent a craft from heeling over from a contrary current or a sudden wind. The journals tell of "banks falling in" as the river undercut the shore, which collapsed into the river, nearly catching the men towing the boats along the shore. Such collapses narrowly missed inundating the boats. The work was both difficult and dangerous.

I recall hunting along the lower Brazos River in Texas during heavy rains the spring of 1950 and hearing explosions. Following the sound to its source, I discovered huge masses of sandy riverbank, undercut by the current, falling into the flooding Brazos with tremendous repercussions.

Isolation

As we look at the big picture, at the long-term hazards of the expedition, what stands out is the isolation endured by members of the party. Their separation from the world they knew and could depend on, from their basic support systems, posed a serious psychological risk. The captains planned an expedition of more than two years, but various delays and underestimation of distances led to a much longer absence. Some of the men were gone for more than three years, a long time to be away from what they knew as civilization. At Fort Clatsop, Lewis wrote of longing for home.

There would be no communication between expedition members and the American frontier, no word following the expedition up the river, and no direct contact with the outside world unless a ship happened to be found at the mouth of the Columbia (it wasn't). There was no way for Jefferson to get word to Lewis and Clark once they left Wood River, and no

Isolation from their homes, from their own kind, and from their own
culture may have been a hazard to the members of the expedition.
The men had never experienced so vast an expanse of open
landscape as they found on the Great Plains.

means for the captains to send word back to the president after they left
Fort Mandan.

Plans to send the white pirogue down the Missouri with news of the expedition and specimens they had gathered were abandoned when water
became too shallow for the keelboat. To lighten the keelboat's burden,
they transferred part of the load to the smaller vessels, which kept going
up the Missouri the spring of 1805 when the keelboat headed back downstream. Only when it reached St. Louis the spring of 1805 did word of the
expedition reach that frontier outpost. President Jefferson did not learn
that fact until several weeks later when he received letters from Lewis.

Their isolation was tempered by the fact that much of the region they
explored was known: the Ohio River Valley was well settled, St. Louis had
a population of roughly a thousand (though few of the men got to visit his
thriving city), and the five Mandan and Hidatsa villages where they wintered on the Upper Missouri probably had a total population of four thousand or more. The Columbia River, too, swarmed with native people, but
Indians were not like "civilized" Americans.

Lewis and Clark kept meeting people on the river: trappers and traders,
employees of the Hudson's Bay Company and the North West Company,

and the hundreds of Indians representing dozens of tribes living in the Missouri watershed. The Columbia River, rich in salmon, sustained thousands of native people. Although many Indians lived along the route the expedition traveled, most of the area was untamed, unfamiliar, even unfriendly. It was an uncivilized wilderness in spite of its numerous indigenous populations.

Separated by hundreds of miles from their homes and country, members of the Lewis and Clark expedition knew isolation. They had each other, but between the Mandan villages and the Columbia River lay a vast wild country full of fish and game, wild fruits, berries, and edible roots, and a massive natural world full of native peoples who thrived on the abundant resources. But it wasn't home, it wasn't the United States, and it wasn't civilized even by frontier standards.

Jefferson's anticipation of this isolation remains the most significant factor in the careful planning that made the expedition possible and led to its success. From the outset, the party had included in its supplies everything it could possibly need plus spare parts and tools to repair whatever they had or to build whatever they required.

The Corps of Discovery included blacksmiths, carpenters, a gunsmith, a tailor, and hunters who kept the party well supplied with meat and with hides for clothing. These items were also traded with the Indians in exchange for food, guide services, and information, especially when the men were off the rivers (on the rivers, they generally knew which way to go and seemed to have plenty to eat). At Fort Mandan, in the winter of 1804–1805, the party's three blacksmiths kept the expedition well fed by making battle-axes for the Mandan warriors in exchange for corn, dried squash, and beans.

While it is true that only one member of the party died, the men of the expedition were often ill, injured, hypothermic, or exhausted. They had no doctor; they were isolated from medical services. However, Lewis and Clark doctored the men with an assortment of home remedies—Rush's pills, Peruvian bark, and frequent bleedings. An Indian sweat bath cured Bratton of his chronic bad back. When Lewis was accidentally shot through the buttocks, he did his best to treat himself; unable to reach the wound, he instructed the men with him in how to treat the injury until they rejoined Clark's party.

The expedition survived remarkably well. They had carried tons of food with them. On the river, they generally ate well; off the river, they nearly starved. But it probably wasn't food or medical care they missed as much as their own culture. They must have felt isolated from civilization as they knew it. The fiddles of Cruzatte and Gibson served as succor, but separation from their known world must have frightened them at times. As fascinating and exotic as their experiences no doubt were, they existed in a foreign place full of potential danger.

The Rivers, Their Currents, and Obstacles

Traveling by river most of the way, the men of the expedition had to learn the ways of the river, had to develop a river sense. They learned to read water, to scout rapids, to judge conflicting currents, and to anticipate crumbling banks and islands being washed away beneath them by the swift current. They made many mistakes, but they learned from them, and they survived thousands of miles of river travel, largely in boats they not only built themselves but repaired to keep afloat and moving on.

Even before they left Wood River in the spring of 1804, the Corps of Discovery came to know rivers. Some of the men had floated down the Ohio in the keelboat and pirogues, and had powered them up the Mississippi the previous autumn. Some had manned the pirogues across the river to St. Louis, carrying Lewis or Clark back and forth with letters, orders, dispatches, and supplies for the coming trip up the Missouri.

Camped near the Mississippi for nearly six months, they saw many kinds of boats traveling upstream and down. They watched the river rise and fall, saw it run with ice and carry debris past their camp. They became familiar with the big river and with their own tiny tributary. They began to sense the implications of their enterprise. They made trial runs, feeling conflicting currents and the force of the river, sensing the power of the Mississippi. In anticipation of the coming venture, they watched the muddy waters of the Missouri pouring into the Father of Waters, imagining the shining mountains where they'd heard the Missouri River began.

Although official orders from Secretary of War Henry Dearborn had called for men experienced on rivers, few of the American soldiers knew rivers as well as any of the French voyageurs hired to man the red pirogue, or Pierre Cruzatte and François Labiche, the point men on the keelboat. Familiar with the river's subtleties, its power, and its quixotic currents, the experienced rivermen served as teachers for the less experienced crew of the keelboat and the white pirogue. On May 15, 1804, their second day heading up the Missouri, Clark wrote, "One of the Perogue are not Sufficiently maned to keep up."[8] Which one do you suppose it was? I'm sure it was the white pirogue manned by the American soldiers.

The French rivermen taught them to read the surface of the water, to examine the river for signs of shoals and hidden obstacles. They taught them to feel the river through their oars and poles, to sense the currents playing against the hull. They schooled the men in how to avoid such obstacles as sawyers, shoals, sleepers, snags, and sweepers.

Rivers continually eat away at their banks, especially during floods. They send great numbers of trees into the river, where they land by quixotic chance and natural law in shallow water or on bars and islands, usually with their root wads pointed upstream. The massive root wad is the heaviest, bulkiest part of the tree and finds bottom first; the tree top, being lighter, continues to float until, brought up short by its anchored root wad, it comes to rest pointing downstream, the direction of the current.

If a treetop hits something before it floats to its downstream position, it may create an obstacle by blocking a route or bridging a channel, an extremely dangerous situation in which the water may carry a craft under the bridge or into the obstacle. Depending on its height above the river level, it may actually sink the craft by sweeping it beneath the hazard.

Tree limbs become strainers, capable of trapping flotsam as well as people under water with the full force of the current holding them there. When an undercut tree falls into the river with its roots still anchored to the bank, the combination poses an especially dangerous hazard. Every river threatens numerous life-endangering situations; the rivers the expedition party followed were no exception. Zadok Cramer listed planters, sawyers and wooded islands as major hazards to navigation, along with bank instability and swift currents rushing out of the river at high water.[9]

LOGJAMS *lie in wait at the head of islands, a mass of wooden debris, including whole trees, lodged at the island's upstream point. As the island splits the current, floating debris sweeps onto this dividing point where huge masses of flotsam remain until the next high water or until they rot away or catch fire and burn. Logjams offer a nasty obstacle for boats heading down river, but they also offer a good supply of firewood for island camping.*

PLANTERS *are tree trunks firmly anchored in the river bottom, too*

Planters are solid tree trunks anchored firmly in the river
bottom. Unseen in muddy water, they can damage a boat.

*large and solid to saw back and forth in the current (like a sawyer) but
capable of knocking a hole in a craft's bottom, damaging a rudder, or
sending the boat off course.*

SAWYERS *are trees of lesser size anchored to the bottom of the river
with their tops, usually pointed downstream, sawing in the current,
up and down, back and forth; they are a serious hazard to boats, even
to steamboats. Mississippi steamboat captain Mark Twain got the
name for one of his most famous characters from this common and
dangerous river feature.*

SHOALS *are shallow places in the riverbed. The expedition encountered them as they drifted down the low-water Ohio in the fall of
1803 and again on the upper Missouri the following two years, especially above the Great Falls.*

SLEEPERS *are broad obstacles barely underwater that cause little
surface disturbance and lie in wait for unsuspecting boats whose lookouts are not paying careful attention; sleepers may capture boats, alter their course, or bash their bottoms.*

SNAGS *are trees, often dead ones, lodged on shallow bars or firmly
anchored to the riverbed, obstacles that occur naturally in most rivers,
the result of eroding shorelines that precipitate trees into the river with
every spring flood or other high-water periods.*

SWEEPERS are trees anchored to the shore but with their tops in the river or slightly above water level, positioned to sweep anything on deck into the river as a boat passes beneath it: sweepsmen, rowers, polers, passengers, the boat's load.

———～～～———

In my forty-five years of guiding on Wyoming's Snake River, I have seen many river accidents: a tree fell across an inflatable raft full of people, pinning the raft and injuring some of its passengers (one died); a small rowing raft, blown into the bank by winds so severe the oarsman could not break back into the current, stalled until well after dark (passengers had to be rescued); a kayaker waited too long to decide which side of an island to take and drowned when his craft was caught beneath a log lodged on the upstream point of the island.

Once, a small raft, manned by four paddlers who failed to make a decision quickly enough, was swept into a logjam; it capsized and all of its passengers were swept beneath the logjam. One of them, caught by underwater tree limbs, drowned. A pontoon drifted into a fallen tree totally blocking a channel (the channel had been clear the previous day; the tree fell during an overnight storm). Fortunately, no one was injured, but all the passengers got wet feet, walking the log to shore.

A dory plowed into a sweeper, its passengers receiving a back scratching as the tree all but swept them out of the craft. A canoe swept into a logjam just like Clark's canoe did on the Beaverhead on June 12, 1806 (see chapter 7, Incidents). The same things that happened to various Lewis and Clark expedition members still happens to boaters today, perhaps multiplied as river running becomes a popular activity.

———～～～———

Natural vegetative hazards lurk dangerously, but rocks and sandbars may "sleep" too, especially in low water, which is slow water. Subtle currents may hide sleepers. Islands become obstacles when they block a boater's view. Boaters must maneuver around them, going to one side or the other or risk running aground on their upstream points or running into the logjams that so often decorate their upstream points.

Bedrock, erosion deposits, exfoliated blocks, and debris flows left by flash floods form rapids that obstruct river channels and divert the main flow. Lewis and Clark observed rock debris brought into the river by tributaries, especially after severe thunderstorms or during spring snowmelt. Most rapids lie at the mouths of these branches. Where a side stream ("drain" in the captains' parlance) floods, it drops rock debris into the main river, temporarily damming the flow and forming a rock garden that we know as a rapid.

Such obstructions were common on the upper Missouri, especially in the Missouri River Breaks, where Clark wrote, "the bad places are verry numerous, i e at the mouth of every Drean [drain] the rocks which is a hard dark gritey Stone is thrown out Some distance in the river which Cause a Considerable riffle on that Side."[10] Such debris flows, as they are called, lie at the mouth of every tributary stream. They create most of the Grand Canyon rapids as well as those on many other rivers.

On the Snake and Columbia Rivers, both of which flow through volcanic landscapes, bedrock rapids are more common. Where the Columbia cuts through the Cascades, its course is beset with bedrock and blocks of basalt that create chutes and falls. These forced the expedition to portage as they traveled both upstream and down. Portaging around the falls and rapids was hard, dangerous work; even lining the boats down tricky chutes taxed the strength of men and their elk-skin towlines.

In the fall of 1805, hurrying to reach the Pacific before winter arrived, the expedition experienced real whitewater for the first time. They ran rapids they should have scouted and bashed boats on rocks, splitting them and perching them on sleepers. They sank boats, soaked the baggage, and swamped canoes in big waves.

Lining (towing) a heavy dugout up the swift current the following spring, they lost it and its load and had to purchase two Indian canoes to replace it. They found the Columbia much higher that spring than it had been the previous autumn. When traveling against the powerful current of the big river became too much for them—when it began to cost them too much time and effort—they abandoned the river and traded for horses to go overland.

Weather

Wherever they traveled, the Corps of Discovery encountered unique weather hazards: thunderstorms with strong, sudden winds, loud rolling thunder, stabbing lightning, and heavy rains that caused flash floods and turned river banks slick with mud; constant rain at the mouth of the Columbia that rotted clothes off their bodies; sub-zero temperatures that frostbit exposed parts; fog that obliterated the river until the sun burned it off; and merciless heat that blistered the backs of the nearly naked men and caused heatstroke. As frontiersmen, the members of the expedition had grown accustomed to working in all kinds of weather, but never before had they experienced such extremes.

They lived with the wind, which normally blew upstream during daylight hours when they did most of their traveling—a tailwind when they traveled upstream and sailed, but a headwind they had to battle when they traveled down river with the flow. The wind often grew too strong for travel; some days it delayed them for hours. Sudden gusts capsized a pirogue more than once, and wind-whipped waves splashed into their dugouts, wetting baggage, food, gifts for the Indians, even powder. The party then had to stop to dry everything, another delay.

Severe winds plague the Columbia River Gorge, a modern mecca for wind surfers but a hassle for the expedition two hundred years ago. Wind drove the boats before it when they sailed, helping them make good mileage, but it also ruffled the water, raising waves the canoes could not deflect or negotiate. The expedition lost several days, pinned down by wind and waves near the mouth of the Columbia.

Thunderstorms on the Great Plains were a new phenomenon to the Corps of Discovery; so were the flash floods that accompanied them. They had known storms at home but none had experienced such strong winds, such violent thunder and lightning, such sudden gusts. Hailstones bloodied the men on the portage around the Great Falls of the Missouri. The crew suffered sunstroke in heat that generated anvil-shaped clouds climbing into the heavens, before all hell broke loose in severe thunderstorms.

In the winter at Fort Mandan, cold winds froze their faces. Ice locked their boats into the river. Hunting the wind-swept prairie, they suffered frostbite to their hands, feet, and faces. They built huts under arctic conditions to protect themselves from the bitter cold. As they traveled in late fall and early spring, water sometimes froze on their oars, adding weight the men didn't need or appreciate. From one extreme to another, they battled the elements that hardened them.

Fire

Fire, another ancient element, became a hazard on at least one occasion. On May 23, 1805, Whitehouse reports, "we halted and made fire to dine at a timbred bottom on N. S. one of the hunters took his rifle & bullitt pouch on Shore the fire broke out into the woods, and burned up his shot pouch powder horn & the stalk of his rifle."[11] One time a tree caught fire and nearly destroyed their tipi. Several times the expedition saw smoke and found recently burned prairie from fires they thought had been set by Indians. They occasionally set fire to the prairie to signal the tribes.

Wildlife

The animals the men of the expedition hunted provided them with food, but wildlife sometimes created serious problems. Hostile grizzly bears attacked the hunters, with or without provocation, and sometimes chased men right into the river, once even swimming after one of them until his companions killed the beast (see chapter 7, Incidents).

As the men towed the boats from the shore they discovered that rattlesnakes abounded. [On a sixty-mile stretch of the upper Missouri in the summer of 2002, I found three rattlesnakes in five days.] One man, seeking a hold as he towed along the brushy shore, grabbed a rattlesnake but released it quickly enough to avoid being bitten. Another, bitten on the ankle on July 4, 1804, survived. The journal keepers commented regularly on the numerous rattlesnakes, more worrisome than hazardous.

One night a stampeding bull buffalo ran through camp, nearly trampling the sleeping men; it ran across one of the pirogues and damaged a rifle that had been left in the boat. Another day they encountered bison swimming the river in a herd so vast they had to stop to avoid being trampled and swamped. While building canoes above the Great Falls, a bull buffalo came to within a few feet of the men but did not charge.

A cornered beaver bit Lewis's dog on the leg, severing an artery; Seaman almost bled to death. Perhaps the most troublesome beasts were the smallest ones—the mosquitoes, flies, gnats, fleas, and lice. The journal writers, especially Clark, wrote of the bothersome mosquitoes. Seaman whimpered all one night because of mosquito bites, and Lewis suffered on bivouac when he forgot his protective mosquito netting.

As pests, flies and gnats came in a poor second. On the lower Columbia,

Rattlesnakes, abundant along the expedition's route, were often encountered by members of the expedition, but only one man was bitten by a snake; he survived with no serious effect. Still the men had to be continually vigilant to avoid snakebite.

Captain Clark—Buffalow Gangue, by John F. Clymer. Reproduced with permission of Mrs. John F. Clymer and the Clymer Museum of Art, Ellensburg, Washington.

where many native people lived in semi-permanent villages, fleas became a great plague. With a rainy and relatively warm climate, the Pacific Northwest rarely gets cold enough weather to zap the fleas between seasons, and with so many people and dogs living so close together, the bloodthirsty creatures thrive. Camping at abandoned Indian villages along the Columbia, the expedition provided the fleas with fresh blood.

Hazardous or merely bothersome, the wildlife the men of the expedition encountered kept them on their toes, prevented them from sleeping, occasionally woke them up at night, and threatened them on numerous occasions. The Corps of Discovery withstood all attacks and threats.

Indians

Natural hazards paled into insignificance in the face of thousands of native people living in the neighborhood. They were sometimes a warlike people who resented the white man's intrusions and feared the diseases that had already decimated some tribes. (The Omaha's powerful Chief Blackbird had died of smallpox just a few years before the expedition passed through; to honor his memory, Lewis and Clark visited his grave.) The native people saw their sources of meat and furs reduced, the balance of power among tribes upset, and their very way of life challenged.

In their speeches to the Indians, Lewis and Clark referred to the native people as "children" and seldom gave them as many gifts as they probably expected from so large and well-provisioned an expedition. In a touchy encounter, the Teton Sioux tried to prevent their going up the Missouri; the situation came near to exploding.[12] Later, four expedition members did battle with a party of Piegan Blackfeet on the headwaters of the Marias. They killed at least one Indian and a second may have died, but the Corps of Discovery avoided any loss of life to Indian attacks.

Although the Americans brought many useful products, such as metal cooking vessels and knives, and fishhooks and guns, many of the tribes' members resented the white man's presence, especially when weighed against a way of life hundreds of years old. Some still do. When I asked Bonnie Jo Hunt, a Teton Sioux singer and storyteller, if her people had any stories about Lewis and Clark, she smiled and demurred, saying, "We were the bad guys to Lewis and Clark." Her people believe the expedition began the decimation of the Sioux and the destruction of their culture.

Similarly, a Lakota woman, who serves as an emergency-room nurse in

Albuquerque, once treated me. When she learned I was writing a book about the Lewis and Clark expedition, she sneered and said under her breath, "Those bastards." Despite Lewis and Clark bicentennial activities that bring together the tribes the Corps of Discovery encountered, many Indian people still harbor negative feelings about the expedition.

Even members of the Nez Perce, the tribe that was closest to the Lewis and Clark expedition, considered killing the members of the expedition once they arrived on the Clearwater, nearly starved after crossing the Bitterroot Mountains. Instead, the tribe fed them salmon, roots, and berries; agreed to care for their horses over the winter; taught them to build canoes; even provided them with a guide for their voyage down the Clearwater, Snake, and Columbia.

Initially, tribal leaders had planned to kill these white men and take their weapons and trade goods. Watkuweis, an elderly Nez Perce woman who had been captured and held as a slave, saved their lives. Some white men had treated her kindly, and she convinced the Nez Perce that the Americans were good men and should not be robbed and killed.

The landscape through which the Lewis and Clark expedition traveled was well populated by numerous Indian tribes, many of them hostile to one another, and some of them hostile to white men in general and to Americans in particular. Indians were a potential hazard but one that rarely materialized. Lewis and Clark's attempt to make peace among the tribes failed, but their promises of future trade interested the Indians enough to appease most of them for the time.

Many hazards threatened the expedition; hazards came with the territory. The captains had anticipated these hazards and planned for them. The men came to expect them. They counted the risks and proceeded on. They lost only one man, killed one Indian, perhaps a second, but they avoided any major attack. They had accidents; men were injured, several suffered from diseases. They survived through illness and injury, isolation and Indian troubles, wildlife and weather to return triumphant, well tempered by the hazards they had faced and successful by most modern standards.

Chapter 4

THE CRAFTS

Of the 10,624 miles the Lewis and Clark expedition logged from Pittsburgh to the Pacific and back to St. Louis, they traveled 9,046 miles by river. That long voyage on many different rivers required a variety of watercrafts. On various river segments they used a keelboat, three pirogues, sixteen dugout canoes, at least five Indian canoes, and a number of skin boats and log rafts. They adapted their crafts to their needs and to the nature of the rivers. When the Missouri became too shallow for the keelboat, they moved much of the load to the smaller pirogues. When the waves at the mouth of the Columbia became too much to manage in dugouts, they traded for Indian canoes.

The streams changed in character as the men climbed the river stairway to the Continental Divide. They confronted their biggest step at the Great Falls of the Missouri, which required an eighteen-mile portage with a 360-foot climb, but by that time they had left both pirogues behind, hoping to replace their carrying capacity with Lewis's skin-covered iron boat. When it failed, they simply built two more dugout canoes.

While the keelboat served as the expedition's workhorse, the dugout canoes they built while on the route did most of the long-term hauling. However, the white pirogue, their smallest craft when they started up the Missouri the spring of 1804, was the largest craft to return to St. Louis in the fall of 1806. Intended to go the shortest distance of all their initial boats, it became the craft that traveled the farthest.

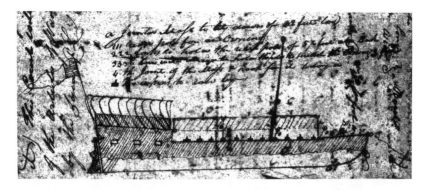

Found in Clark's Field Notes discovered in 1953, this side-view
sketch of the expedition's keelboat, dated January 21, 1804, shows
eleven blocks with thole pins mounted on the gunnel along with a
key to explain the various features of his sketch ("T is pins to
row by"). They seem to indicate eleven sets of double-banked
oars used to power the keelboat up the Missouri.

The Keelboat

Although the keelboat has come to symbolize the expedition, they used
it to travel only one-fifth of their total distance, and for much of that
distance it carried little or no cargo.[1] They employed it for less than six
months (May 14, 1804, to November 2, 1804) to haul the massive load of
equipment and provisions to their advanced base camp at Fort Mandan,
but the keelboat drew too much water to be used on the upper Missouri.
It was sent back to St. Louis in the spring of 1805.

The expedition started out in Pittsburgh where the keelboat was built,
where their trip by water began, and where Meriwether Lewis first wrote
in his journal. While the keelboat ultimately served as their major freight-
hauling craft, it carried little on its maiden voyage down the Ohio the
fall of 1803. Three pirogues augmented the keelboat's limited carrying
capacity on a shallow river that autumn. During 1804 it took them only as
far as the Mandan villages, where they spent the winter of 1804–1805.

The keelboat returned to St. Louis in the spring of 1805, manned by
a skeleton crew. It carried important letters, a variety of faunal and floral
specimens, and a few live creatures; then it disappeared from history. The
permanent party continued upriver toward the western ocean in two pirogues and six dugout canoes they had built at Fort Mandan.

A replica of the Lewis and Clark keelboat, built by Butch Bouvier
of Onawa, Iowa, shows its basic profile, captains' quarters at stern
with awning-covered steering deck, and mast (smaller mast
belongs to pirogue behind keelboat).

The Ohio River originates in Pittsburgh at the confluence of the Allegheny and Monongahela Rivers, an ideal spot to gather equipment and
supplies for the expedition and a logical location to build a keelboat intended to haul everything downstream to the heart of the Midwest where
the full expedition actually began at a base camp on the Mississippi.

The keelboat would be used to carry several tons of gear and provisions
down the Ohio, up the Mississippi to the expedition's Camp Wood near
St. Louis, then up the Missouri—a daunting task against the river's strong
current. Keelboat traffic was common on those big western rivers, traveling both upstream and down on a sporadic basis.

Built that summer by an inebriated boatwright whose excessive drinking delayed the expedition for nearly two months, the keelboat had been
ordered for completion in early July. Lewis found the boat builder drunk
and guilty of "unpardonable negligence." The launch date changed to
August 1, then to August 8, as Lewis fumed at the delay. The boat wasn't
finished until the end of August. Lewis, with a crew of ten men and a river

A steering deck covered with an awning roofs the captains' quarters.
The cleated walkway for poling is formed by the locker lids. Poles
attached to the side and the tiller handle are also visible.

pilot, finally launched the craft three hours after the final nail was driven
into its outer shell on the last day of August.

The keelboat was fifty-five feet long and eight feet wide (Both David
Lavender and Richard C. Boss write of "an 8-foot 4-inch beam."[2]) Empty,
it drew three feet of water; fully loaded, four feet. It had an adjustable
thirty-two-foot mast supporting a large square sail and rigging for a foresail. It had twenty-two rowing spaces—eleven rowing benches when refitted at Camp Dubois—and a sturdy internal keel. The craft included
two ten-foot-long decks, one at the bow, the other at the stern. The ele-
vated stern deck held a small cabin for the captains, who frequently referred to the keelboat as *the Boat*. Lewis often called it a *bateau*, a craft
common along the Ohio and Mississippi Rivers. It was also known simply
as *the barge*.

It was equipped for four means of propulsion: a large square sail for sailing, twenty-two oars and thole pins "to row by," a supply of push poles for
poling or pushing, and several ropes for towing. It could be sailed when
the wind was right; rowed by a large crew of strong men; poled by a co-

ordinated team; or towed by oxen, horses, or men. The crew members often served as beasts of burden; traveling down the Ohio on low water, they literally had to lift the boat over shoals on numerous occasions.

A rudder at the rear helped steer the keelboat. Lockers for luggage and gear lined each side, their lids forming a catwalk inside the gunnel for poling. Because the locker lids prevented the oar looms (handles) from being lowered enough for the blades to clear the waves, thole pins were set on raised wooden blocks. Clark's side-view sketch of the keelboat shows eleven such thole pin mounts; a note above the sketch indicates their purpose: "T in pins to row by," with a separate sketch of a single thole pin set on a block.

Intended to haul heavy equipment and supplies from the industrial East to the expedition's Midwestern starting point, the keelboat had a thirty-one-foot hold theoretically capable of carrying twelve tons. In his article, "Keelboat, Pirogue, and Canoe: Vessels Used by the Lewis and Clark Corps of Discovery,"[3] Boss calculated the keelboat's carrying capacity at twelve to fourteen tons, but Dayton Duncan, in *Out West*,[4] suggests it actually carried only about seven tons. Boss calculated that the two pirogues could carry an additional seventeen tons between them.

The supplies and equipment included fifteen flintlock long-barreled, muzzle-loading rifles of .54 caliber; three dozen metal pipe tomahawks; four large-bore "blunderbusses" (see photo on page 53) or shotguns; fishing gigs (tridents); and the iron boat frame, all from the U.S. Arsenal at Harper's Ferry. The fifty-two powder kegs made of shot lead and filled with imported powder were purchased elsewhere. The load included numerous other items and supplies, mostly food: barrels of pork, corn, flour, salt, and whiskey.

Because the keelboat was finished so late in the season and the river was low, Lewis had difficulty just floating it down the Ohio River empty. He hired wagons and bought pirogues to haul the equipment to Wheeling, Virginia (this corner of Virginia didn't become West Virginia until 1863 in the middle of the Civil War). He also rented horses and oxen to drag the empty boat over the riffles of the Ohio, which was at the lowest water level anyone had seen for four years—it was the end of a drought summer. At several points the crew lifted the keelboat over shoals, manhandling it down the Ohio, a prelude to the hard labor they would frequently experience on the upper Missouri.

At 11 A.M. on August 31, with his party of eleven men plus a Newfound-land dog named Seaman, Lewis left Pittsburgh on the new keelboat. His crew included seven soldiers, a pilot, and three volunteers hopeful of be-ing added to the permanent party. Although their names were not given, George Shannon, the youngest member of the party, and John Colter were thought to have been among them. The undermanned craft made ten miles the first day. Lewis had purchased a leaky pirogue to help carry equipment since the keelboat could haul little. The next day he rented oxen from local farmers to pull the keelboat down the Ohio. There was little current; they made ten more miles.

Each day they struggled with the keelboat in the shallow water and hired more oxen or horses to make progress. They bought a second pi-rogue for eleven dollars (September 4), but it too proved leaky, wetting supplies and delaying the party, which had to stop to dry some goods, in-cluding gifts for the Indians, and to oil rusting guns. It took them eight days to cover the hundred miles to Wheeling, where they bought a third larger pirogue (September 8) and laid over for two days.

Below Wheeling the river was deeper with a slight current. They began making good headway: twenty-four miles the first day, twenty-six the sec-ond. On their second day out of Wheeling, Lewis's dog, Seaman, provided dinner: leaping into the Ohio, he capture several squirrels migrating across the river and brought them back to his new master. Great flocks of mi-grating passenger pigeons filled the sky (a century later, they were almost gone—the last of them died in captivity in 1914).

Through a narrow chute on the north side, with the help of the hired pilot, the men successfully negotiated the Falls of the Ohio, a long rapid with a drop of twenty-four feet over two miles. This rapid lay between Clarksville, Ohio, on the north bank, and Louisville, Kentucky, on the south bank. William Clark and York, with a party of seven volunteers, joined Lewis at Clarksville. At Fort Massac on the lower Ohio, George Drouillard, one of the most experienced frontiersmen of the West and one of the best boatmen in the permanent party, joined them with eight more volunteers; only two of the volunteers were accepted by Lewis and Clark for the permanent party. The captains were becoming carefully selective.

At the confluence of the Ohio with the Mississippi, the party stopped on the point between the two rivers to practice using their various mea-suring instruments. They found the Ohio River 1,274 yards wide, the

Mississippi above the confluence 1,435 yards wide, and the combined flow of the Mississippi below the confluence, 2,002 yards (more than a mile) wide. They crossed the Mississippi to the west (Spanish) side, then (November 20) for the first time turned upstream toward St. Louis and the mouth of the Missouri.

The heavy keelboat had to maneuver back and forth across the river, catching eddies (upstream currents) to make any headway against the powerful flow. They made only ten and a half miles in eight hours of rowing and towing. One man had to keep constant vigil to watch for and ward off floating debris. The twenty-five as-the-crow-flies miles to Cape Girardeau, forty-eight miles by river, took the keelboat four days. As a result, the two captains decided to double the number of men they would need for the expedition up the Missouri. They required more manpower.

The question might be raised, since the river route was longer, why did the expedition use boats instead of taking a shorter overland route? In part, because roads were bad or nonexistent. Hauling fifty-four thousand pounds of equipment and supplies (Boss's estimate) would have required more than five hundred horses and mules, a long pack string. Because Indians were known to steal horses (and did several times during the journey when the expedition resorted to horseback travel) but had never been known to steal a keelboat or pirogue, the water route seems logical.

As mentioned in chapter 3, the main reason they went by water was that President Thomas Jefferson sent the expedition not to explore the Louisiana Territory but to find a commercially feasible water route to the Pacific. Since river travel at that time offered the most practical means of hauling heavy loads over long distances, he ordered them to go by water, to follow the Missouri River as far as they could, then find a connecting river that flowed to the Pacific—if there was one.

The trip down the Ohio and up the Mississippi had served as a training run and shakedown cruise for the keelboat. Clark, the better riverman, became the head boatman once he joined the expedition at Louisville. He used the winter at their base camp to refit the big boat for the trip up the

Missouri and to train the men, to keep them busy preparing for the spring upriver run. During the winter of 1803–1804 at Camp Wood, the keelboat did little traveling. The men revamped the barge, building eleven rowing benches and adding lockers along the sides: two and a half feet wide, one and a half feet deep, with a hinged cover. The locker covers, when raised, served as a shield in case of Indian attack. When closed, the locker covers provided a catwalk along both sides of the keelboat from which the men could pole the heavy craft.

A *discrepancy exists in the record as to just how many oars were used to man the keelboat. At least once they tested it on the Mississippi, using twenty oars, but that was before two French rivermen joined the keelboat crew. Clark wrote on May 13, 1804, that "all our provisions goods and equipage [are] on Board of a Boat of 22 oars."[5] Further evidence of the twenty-two oars appears in Clark's letter of April, 1810, to Nicholas Biddle during his editing of the journals: he writes of "rowing 22 oars."[6]*

The journals state that eleven rowing benches were installed, and Clark's side-view sketch of the keelboat clearly shows eleven thole pins and thole-pin mounts on the gunnel, even though his plan-view sketch shows only twenty oars. My guess would be that it was designed for twenty-two oars but they may have used twenty or fewer much of the time.

Boss says, "the 31-foot hold was fitted with ten thwarts to pull twenty double-banked oars."[7] I assume that by "thwarts" he means rowing benches, but the journals say eleven rowing benches. "Double-banked" means that two rowers sat side-by-side, each pulling an oar (in contrast to single-banked oars, in which the oars were alternated, one on the left, the next one on the right, not used in pairs).

They had planned to leave Camp Wood on April 18, but were delayed. On May 8, on a trial run up the Mississippi, they learned that the keelboat was loaded too heavily in the bow, and they had to shift more cargo to the stern. When they finally left Camp Wood on May 14, 1804, they crossed the Mississippi and headed up the Missouri, making roughly six miles:

one and a half miles across the Mississippi and four and a half miles up the Missouri. Now they found the stern too heavily loaded.

The next day they made ten miles; the white pirogue lagged behind. The third day they "set sail" at 5 A.M., reaching St. Charles on the north bank by 2 P.M. Here they again adjusted the cargo, placing more in the bow. They also took on additional supplies. Then they waited for Lewis to arrive from St. Louis, where he had last-minute business.

St. Charles was a river town, populated by French voyageurs. The captains hired two of them, Cruzatte and Labiche. The crew mingled with the local residents, went to church, and got drunk. They were getting to know both the keelboat and the river as they prepared to say farewell to civilization for what would prove to be more than two years.

The day they left St. Charles (May 22) they made eighteen miles under a following wind, a good day for the upriver voyage. The keelboat crew at this time included twenty-two rowers and three sergeants, plus Lewis and Clark, York, and the Newfoundland dog, Seaman. The water was rapid, the "banks falling in," undercut by the swift current. They needed to overpower the current to make headway. We don't know what techniques they used on a given day unless one of the journal keepers tells us; often none did. The journals of Whitehouse and Ordway provided the best data about their means of powering the crafts.

The journals often say they "set sail," but almost certainly they also manned the oars, all twenty-two of them at times. They obviously "rowed and towed," but the journals provide little detail except on rare occasions. Running too close to shore on June 5, 1804, the keelboat mast broke when the craft passed beneath a stout overhanging sycamore branch; consequently, they had no sail to take advantage of a good following wind later that day. June 17, 1804, though the captains' journals fail to tell us how they powered the crafts, they obviously towed, for they broke the tow rope. (For techniques, see chapter 6.)

It seems appropriate at this point to mention the organization of the keelboat crew. Three sergeants served on a rotating basis in three positions: (1) one at the bow to look out for obstacles, to ward off any potentially damaging debris (floating logs, whole trees, dead buffalo), to watch for game and Indians, and to keep in touch with the pirogues; (2) one at the mast to manage the sail, command the guard, oversee the rowers, and watch for special features of the landscape (river mouths, geological phenomena, key landmarks); and (3) one at the helm to steer, to manage deck baggage, to attend the compass, and to assist Clark with his map-making duties. Each day as they changed the guard, the sergeant at the helm (stern) moved to the middle of the keelboat; the one at the middle moved to the bow; and the one at the bow moved to the stern.

The keelboat was the workhorse of the expedition, and the men on the keelboat became beasts of burden, even being harnessed to tow the "barge," working as hard as humanly possible to haul the heavy craft up-stream: rowing, poling, towing, sailing when the wind allowed. They used the keelboat to carry their gear and supplies for only six months, mid-May to early November, 1804, but it hauled massive amounts of equipment, provisions, and trade goods to what might be called their advanced base camp at Fort Mandan. Since the keelboat carried so little on its trip down the Ohio, it could hardly be said to have been of practical use before it headed up the Missouri from Camp Wood.

In the spring of 1805, again with a skeleton crew, the keelboat returned to St. Louis, carrying a collection of bones, skulls, skins, plants, seeds, and a few live creatures: a sharp-tailed grouse, a prairie dog, and four magpies. The journals say little about the downriver run (the journal writers had all gone upriver as part of the permanent party), but we know from other sources that it took forty-five days to make the sixteen hundred miles to St. Louis, where the keelboat arrived on May 21, 1805. Without the keel-boat to haul their heaviest equipment and supplies to Fort Mandan, the expedition would never have succeeded. Even though the keelboat was used for only a few months and gave them more trouble than any other craft, it served its purpose well and made the expedition possible.

The Pirogues

Two pirogues helped carry the party and its equipment and supplies from their base camp at Wood River to their advanced base camp at the Man-dan villages in present-day North Dakota. The same two crafts plus six canoes, which the men had carved out of cottonwood logs near their win-ter camp, carried the expedition up the Missouri the next spring. Neither pirogue was portaged around the Great Falls. One, cached at the Marias mouth, failed to survive the winter. The other helped the Corps of Discov-ery return to St. Louis in the fall of 1806. Above Fort Mandan, the pirogues replaced the keelboat as the expedition's workhorse on the Missouri.

The word *pirogue* was rarely spelled correctly in the journals kept by members of the expedition, though it was spelled at least thirteen different ways. Pirogue (PEE-row) is a Caribbean Indian word that came into the English language through Spanish and French. It originally referred to a canoe made by hollowing out a large log, but it eventually came to mean any canoe-shaped boat. In the days of Lewis and Clark it often meant a long narrow boat built of planks.

Journal writers confused matters by using the terms "pirogue" and "canoe" interchangeably. None of them described the pirogues except to designate a larger red one manned by seven oars; the other, smaller and white, was manned by six oars. Clark left us a single sketch of the white pirogue in his field notes but offered no dimensions.

I concur with the opinion that Stephen Ambrose advanced in *Undaunted Courage:* the pirogues used by the Lewis and Clark expedition were "probably big flat-bottomed masted row boats built from planks."[8] In his February, 1993, article in *We Proceeded On,* Arlen J. Large states that the red pirogue was "a flat-bottomed, single-masted boat made from planks and rowed with seven oars."[9]

In his 1993 article about the boats used by the Corps of Discovery, Richard Boss, a nautical engineer, wrote, "the Party's pirogues were not dugouts," based in part on the fact that they had rudder irons and therefore did not require a steering oar. He also stated that they used single-banked oars, that is, single oars used alternately rather than side-by-side paired oars—there wouldn't have been room in the narrow pirogues for double-banked oars.[10] Don Holm, in his contribution to the Western Writers' *Water Trails West,* refers to pirogues as "typical flat-bottomed, planked, canoe-type river boats."[11]

Journal evidence suggests that planks were repaired and indicates that when the party abandoned the red pirogue at the mouth of the Marias on their return from the Pacific, they removed nails and other iron fittings. We know little of the pirogues used by the expedition, for the journals provide few specific details and only one sketch by Clark, which tells us very little.[12]

Lewis had purchased three pirogues in the fall of 1803 as the party traveled down the Ohio River to winter camp on the Mississippi. We are never told which of the three—or for that matter, if any of them—were used to travel up the Missouri. All we know is that the Corps used two pirogues; that one was red and the other white; that one had seven oars and the other, six; and that each pirogue had a mast, a sail, and a rudder.

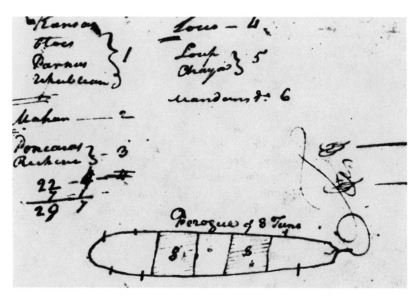

William Clark's April 12, 1804, sketch of the white pirogue shows
six tic-marks on the gunnel, four fore and two aft, suggesting rowing
positions. The white pirogue was manned by six oars.

We don't know the exact size of the pirogues. At one point Lewis had
planned to use a forty-foot pirogue to augment the keelboat's carrying
capacity. Historian Jim Hendrix, headmaster of the Lovette School in
Atlanta and a Lewis and Clark scholar, told me that his professor in grad-
uate school at Louisiana State University, John Loos, whom they called
"meticuloos" for his detailed accuracy, told him that the pirogues were a
twenty-five-footer and a thirty-footer. Hendrix doesn't know where Loos
got that information, nor have I found any specifics in my own research.

The pirogue purchased in Wheeling was "a large craft," but we don't
know how large or what color—or for certain that it was used to go up the
Missouri. Some Lewis and Clark scholars believe it was the red pirogue,
but I have found no evidence to prove the point. Typical pirogues in use
on the Ohio River at the time were often fifty or more feet long but only
five feet wide, according to David Lavender.[13]

They were sometimes paired in a catamaran arrangement with deck-
ing to hold them together and to increase their carrying capacity. Although
the expedition did not use such an arrangement with their pirogues, they
did lash two canoes together for the return trip down the Yellowstone and
Missouri.

Butch Bouvier's replica of the white pirogue at Lewis and Clark
State Park in Onawa, Iowa, suggests its eight-ton carrying capacity and
illustrates several means of power and control (sailing, rowing, poling).

The pirogues became invaluable to the expedition for ferrying men
and supplies across the river, for scouting upstream and exploring tributaries, for hauling meat to camp, and for special details. During their
struggle up the Missouri to the Mandan villages, the Corps of Discovery
often left one of the pirogues behind to haul meat to camp and to bring up
a party member who became lost or was delayed. They did not yet have
the smaller canoes to serve that purpose.

On the upper Missouri a pirogue was used for hauling stones to Fort
Mandan to build the chimney for their winter camp. A pirogue may have
been used for warping, for on June 21, 1804, Sergeant Gass wrote in his
journal, "for about a mile [we] had to warp up our boat by rope." If they
had indeed warped the keelboat, they may have used a pirogue to carry
the rope upstream before tying it to a tree. Clark's entry for the day states
simply, "Sometimes rowing, Poling and Drawing up with a Strong Rope
we assended without wheeling or receiving damage." The drawing up
with a strong rope sounds much like warping, a technique for winching a
boat upstream with a windless on board.

THE RED PIROGUE. The red pirogue, the larger of the two pirogues that took the expedition up the Missouri, was as much as thirty-five to forty-five feet long and five to seven feet wide, according to educated guesses by experts. Manned by experienced rivermen, it usually made better time than the smaller white pirogue. At one point, "the French rund a Snag thro: [their pirogue] and she like to have Sunk."[14] They considered sending the damaged boat back to St. Louis with dispatches, but they apparently repaired it and kept going.

As many as eleven French rivermen are listed as its crew, but some names appear on the roster only once and names were added or dropped as the expedition moved up the river. Many French rivermen lived along the banks of the Missouri. The crew probably never topped eight or nine at any one time; Clark's July 4, 1804, roster lists eight men including the river boss. A careless lot, they paid little attention to keeping their load dry; the party often had to stop to dry wet goods.

The patroon (river boss) was no doubt at the rudder (helm), but he also served as lookout even though he was in no position to respond to danger at the bow. In an emergency, the patroon would send the bowsman (the oarsman nearest the bow) to the bow with a pole to ward off obstacles that might harm the craft or send it off course.

When they traveled upstream, the bow pointed upstream, and the rowers faced downstream, putting their strong backs into pulling the oars. Men looking downstream could not have served as lookouts, nor was the helmsman in position to react quickly enough to save the craft from disaster in an emergency. The bowsman had to do that job and quickly.

The red pirogue was often used to ferry men across the river, but the journals fail to designate precisely which pirogue was used for what activity, especially before the party reached their winter camp at the Mandan villages. This is probably due to the fact that all the journal writers were usually on the keelboat. Sometimes the specific pirogue can be determined by who is rowing or riding in it at the time. The better-manned red pirogue usually served to wait for stragglers or hunters because its crew could catch up with the upstream party much better than the white pirogue manned by the American soldiers.

We know that the red pirogue did not reach the Great Falls of the Missouri nor did it return to St. Louis with the party. Hidden in the woods on an island at the mouth of the Marias River, it decayed over the winter of 1805–1806. When the party returned in the spring of 1806, they found it beyond repair and abandoned it. They removed its nails and other iron works, and then proceeded on down river with the white pirogue and five dugout canoes. The red pirogue was no longer needed. The party had much less to carry on the way back to the United States than they had to haul up the Missouri to supply the Corps of Discovery.

THE WHITE PIROGUE. Bob Saindon, in a 1976 paper presented at the eighth annual meeting of the Lewis and Clark Trail Heritage Foundation, Inc., stated that the white pirogue "was built of poplar wood."[15] Large states in his 1995 article, based in part on Saindon's earlier paper, "The white pirogue was made of popular planks and rowed with six oars."[16] The ultimate source of this information lies in Clark's journal entry for February 28, 1805, when he writes, "got the poplar perogue out of the ice" at Fort Mandan. We know it is the smaller (white) pirogue because the next day they free "the [keel]boat & large perogue from the ice."[17]

In the early planning stage for the expedition, the white pirogue was to have been sent back to St. Louis with letters, documents, and specimens from somewhere upriver. However, when the red pirogue was damaged, and again when the water became too shallow for the keelboat on the upper Missouri, part of the loads of the keelboat and the red pirogue were shifted to the white pirogue, which became indispensable. The keelboat, rather than the white pirogue, was sent back in the spring of 1805. The white pirogue, drawing less water, continued up the Missouri.

Clark's sketch of the white pirogue in his field notes for April 13, 1804, shows six small marks at the gunnels, four fore and two aft. I take them to indicate oar positions, four in front of the forward cargo compartment and two behind the rear one. They are staggered, offset, (not set opposite to one another) giving the men room to row with single-banked oars in the relatively narrow craft.

David Cain, who has rowed Glen Bishop's replica of the white pirogue, believes the men rowed from a standing position, the only way they could row, given the probable inboard length of the oars and the narrow width of the pirogue. If they used fourteen-foot oars, four feet inboard and ten feet outboard, they'd have to stand near the left gunnel to pull an oar attached to the right gunnel.

The white pirogue was the lesser vessel on the way to winter camp at the Mandan villages. It was generally slower. Manned by a U.S. Army crew under Corporal Richard Warfington's command, the craft had six oars and no relief rowers. Warfington was at the rudder when they were on the river; someone else had to ward off obstacles. Since rowers faced downstream, I suspect that when Warfington saw a problem, he ordered the bow rower to grab a pole and protect the craft.

Can you imagine the ribbing the crew of the white pirogue took from the older, more experienced boatmen of the red pirogue? Even though Secretary of War Henry Dearborn had sent orders to western military posts to provide the expedition with men who understood rowing a boat, initially the soldiers were a relatively inexperienced crew. They learned quickly and became excellent boatman before ice shut down the river during the fall of 1804.

The second summer, traveling above Fort Mandan, the white pirogue, considered the safer, more stable craft, became the "queen of the fleet" on the upper Missouri. The French voyageurs had left the party. The members of the permanent party, including Cruzatte and Labiche, now manned the pirogues. The men had learned a great deal about river travel on their way to the Mandan villages, but the men who had maneuvered and powered the pirogues to Fort Mandan had all left the party—except Robert Frazer, who replaced one of the expelled members.

Above their winter camp at Fort Mandan, the white pirogue usually carried Lewis and Clark, York, Charbonneau and Sacagawea with her baby (Pompey), Drouillard (if he wasn't on shore hunting), and three non-swimming privates. None of the party ever wore any kind of life jacket; they hadn't been invented yet.

The white pirogue carried them all the way to the foot of the Great Falls, where it was cached over the winter of 1805–1806 and recovered the following summer. On June 16, 1805, Lewis wrote, "We determined to leave the white pirogue at this place, and substitute the Iron boat."[18] On June 18, 1805, he wrote, "This morning I employed all hands in drawing the pirogue on shore in a thick bunch of willow bushes; . . . fastener her securely, drove out the plugs of the gage holes of her bottom [further evidence of the craft's being a plank boat] and covered her with bushes and driftwood to shelter her from the sun."[19]

Saindon pointed out in his 1976 paper that "The White Pirogue, smallest craft of the flotilla at the onset was the largest at the completion," and that "she was to travel the shortest distance, yet she by far travelled the farthest."[20]

The white pirogue served the expedition well, but we have no real description of it, not even in words from the journals. Our best bet is to examine Clark's sketch of the white pirogue and other boats from the same period. Several Lewis and Clark aficionados have built replica pirogues. Some of these replicas reside in museums; others are used periodically on the Missouri in Lewis and Clark re-enactments.

The Canoes and Other Small Crafts

The word *canoe* came into the English language through Spanish from the Caribbean Indian name for a narrow, lightweight boat made from a hollowed log, normally powered and controlled by paddles or poles. Its sides meet in a blunt edge at each end. The term, first used in the western world by Christopher Columbus in 1493, refers to any long, narrow, bark or skin boats as well as dugouts carved from wood.

The canoes used by the members of the Lewis and Clark expedition were true dugouts. At Fort Clatsop National Historic Site, I found a ten-step description for building a dugout canoe. First find a large straight log and use the butt end as the bow. (Lummi Indians near Bellingham, Washington, would add: the tree must be female and want to be a canoe.) If possible, float the log before you start cutting to determine its natural balance. When carving the log, remove less than you think is necessary. Canoe length is seven to eight times its width, and depth is half to two-thirds its width. The ten steps:

1. Position log on blocks, off the ground, top side up.
2. Debark log to prevent bug infestation and rot.
3. Remove top section until flat. Make cross-cuts with saw, then chunk off with wedges and maul. Use ax or adz to flatten top.
4. Dig out interior conservatively, no more than halfway down.
5. Roll canoe upside down and remove remaining bark.
6. Flatten bottom, parallel to top, half the canoe width.
7. Shape bottom, blending bottom to sides, slope bow and stern.
8. Carefully roll canoe upside up.
9. Dig out canoe to desired thickness (extra thickness at bottom will help stabilize canoe in water), thin to desired thickness.
10. Complete final shaping, round gunnels as desired.

Modern day canoeists, members of the Missouri Department of
Conservation, paddle a cottonwood dugout they built for a
Lewis and Clark reenactment. Courtesy Missouri Department
of Conservation.

The expedition men built a total of sixteen dugout canoes. During
their overland route, when pressed for watercrafts to use for crossing
streams, to haul game to camp, to speed up their travels or respond to
emergencies, they used log rafts and skin boats made of willow frames
covered with buffalo hides. Several times they borrowed or rented Indian
crafts to cross rivers; they built boats of native design, using Indian methods. On the Columbia River they traded with natives for their superior
lightweight, maneuverable canoes.

East of the Divide the expedition members made canoes from cottonwood trees cut green and hollowed out by adz and ax; west of the Divide
they made them from ponderosa pine and hollowed them by burning.
Five times they built canoes: near their winter camp at Fort Mandan in
February–March, 1805 (six canoes); at the top of the Great Falls portage
when the iron boat failed in the summer of 1805 (two canoes); on the
Clearwater River's south bank across from that river's North Fork in the
fall of 1805 (five canoes); again on the Clearwater at what is now called
Camp Chopunnish in the spring of 1806 (one canoe); and Clark's party on
the Yellowstone in July, 1806 (two canoes lashed together as a catamaran).

On the Clearwater River, for the first time, the expedition used fire for hollowing out canoes. Burning out the cottonwood canoes would have been ineffective, because green cottonwood does not burn well. On the Clearwater they used ponderosa pine, which burns nicely. After the party had nearly starved crossing the Bitterroot Mountains, the men were sick and weak, too exhausted to work, but they were obliged to build canoes to continue their journey—and they were in a hurry. Only here did they burn out the core of the canoes, using a technique they learned from the Nez Perce Indians.

At their winter camp at Fort Mandan, Clark's journal entry for February 28, says, "Sent out 16 men to make four Perogus [meaning canoes]."[21] On March 9, he wrote, "Found them [canoes] nearly finished, the timber verry bad."[22] He made no mention to reconcile the fact that six canoes were built (not four). The trees they used were found five or six miles upstream from Fort Mandan and one and a half miles from the river. The canoes were between twenty-five and thirty-five feet long, heavy beasts with thick walls. Once they were finished, the men spent two days hauling them to the river. The party returned to St. Louis in some of these same dugouts.

At the head of the Great Falls portage when the iron boat failed, the expedition built two more canoes from cottonwood trees they found in a grove upstream, eight miles by land, more than twenty-three miles by river. Clark wrote (July 10, 1805), "found two Trees which I thought would make canoes, had them fallen, one of them proved to be hollow & Spilt at one End & verry win shaken at the other, the other much win shaken [wind shaken means cracked with separation between growth rings of trees caused by high winds]."[23] They had to use them nonetheless. While ten men under Clark worked on the canoes, Lewis supervised others in caching supplies and gear they had no craft capacity to carry. Then they ferried their supplies and trade goods to the new canoe site. Soon they were off again up the Missouri to the Three Forks in eight canoes.

On September 25, 1804, on the Clearwater (Kooskooskee) River in the Columbia River watershed, Clark observed, as he walked through a narrow pine bottom, "I saw fine timber for Canoes."[24] Two days later he wrote, "all the men able to work comened building 5 Canoes."[25] Working fast, given their physical state, and using fire to burn out the heart of the trees, the men finished the canoes by October 6. On October 7, Clark wrote, "all the canoes in the water, we Load and Set out, after fixing all our Poles."[26]

A replica of the two canoes the expedition built on the Yellowstone River and lashed together as a catamaran is displayed at Pompey's Pillar, which the expedition passed on July 25, 1806.

On October 8, a canoe split on a rock, filled with water, and sank but was salvaged and repaired. How do you repair a split cottonwood canoe? The journals don't tell us, but the Corps was in conifer country now. Perhaps they used resin or animal skins, but the water would have kept hide patches wet. Perhaps they used the tin sheets, hammer, and nails they had hauled over the Divide. They usually had everything they needed in the way of equipment and tools on this well-planned expedition.

And so it went, down the Clearwater to the Snake, down the Snake to the Columbia, and down the Columbia to the Pacific. When they reached the lower Columbia, they saw Native American canoes for the first time, lightweight maneuverable works of art, products of fine craftsmanship. They traded their smallest canoe for one of the native crafts. During the winter at Fort Clatsop, the tide occasionally took one or another of their canoes, but they usually found them after a few days or even a few weeks.

At their winter lodge near the river's mouth, they traded for another Indian craft. Then, rationalizing that the Indians had stolen food and equipment over the winter, they stole another native craft. They left their winter quarters in three of the old dugouts built on the Clearwater and three Indian canoes: one Clatsop, one Cathlamet, and one Chinook. Half way up their Columbian course they traded for two more native canoes before they left the river on horseback.

On their return to the Clearwater they once again used the burn and chip method for hollowing out a single dugout canoe from ponderosa pine. They needed it for ferrying across the river to hunt and trade with the Nez Perce while they waited for the Bitterroot snow to melt so they could head home. Knowing the technique and being stronger and healthier, they finished a single canoe in record time, but a few days later they lost it: a swift snowmelt current swept it under a logjam. Local Indians helped them recover it a week later, just days before the expedition left the area, its total use limited to a few days.

The final canoes were built on the Yellowstone River by members of the Clark party that had gone overland by horseback from the Three Forks. Upon reaching the Yellowstone (near present-day Livingston, Montana), they traveled downstream for four days before finding trees suitable for building canoes. On July 20, Clark wrote, "fell the two trees which I intended for the two Canoes."[27]

The two canoes they hacked out of cottonwood trees were "28 feet in length and about 16 or 18 inches deep and from 16 to 24 inches wide." By noon three days later the canoes were finished. The men then set out to make oars (probably paddles) and poles, and to hunt. Next morning (July 24) Clark wrote, "had all our baggage put on board of the Small Canoes which when lashed together is very Study and, I am Convinced will [carry] the party I intend takeing down with me."[28]

They had a problem with the catamaran: water between the two hulls splashed into the canoes, wetting their contents. Always resourceful, they stretched buffalo hides from one inside gunnel to the other to deflect the waves and keep the water out of the canoes. They made excellent time in the catamaran craft: sixty-nine and a half miles the first day (July 24); fifty-eight miles the second (July 25), during which they stopped to explore Pompey's Pillar; sixty-two miles the third (July 26); and eighty and a half on July 27. In eight days they covered 488 miles, not bad for the heavy rig. At Buffalo Shoals, a bad stretch with a three-foot drop, they carefully "let the Canoes down by hand for fear of their Striking a rock under water and Splitting."[29] They'd learned not to test their crafts and skills.

Canoes proved the most versatile crafts used on the entire expedition,

A replica of the iron boat is on exhibit at the museum at Camp
Wood River near St. Louis. A great idea, the boat failed to function
because the expedition did not have the proper caulking material.

not only on the smaller rivers but on the Columbia and Snake and on the
Missouri as well. They built them on the spot when they needed them.
These primitive crafts served them well.

THE IRON BOAT. The metal frame for a craft designed by Lewis, the *Experiment*, was built by Army Arsenal personnel at Harper's Ferry at the confluence of the Shenandoah and the Potomac Rivers, the same place the
party obtained their .54 caliber rifles. The craft had a collapsible iron frame
that weighed ninety-nine pounds and folded to four feet in length. Un-
folded and covered with animal skins, it was thirty-six feet long with a
thirty-two-foot keel; it was four feet, three inches wide and would serve,
Lewis calculated, to replace the pirogues for hauling gear and supplies
upstream above the Great Falls.

For days the men had hunted, killing elk and buffalo to supply skins
necessary to cover the boat's iron frame. The men spent hours burning
and scraping the hair off, then sewing the hides together, twenty-eight
elk skins and four buffalo hides. The skin boat, caulked with a mixture
of charcoal, beeswax, and buffalo tallow, initially floated like a cork. Five

The bullboat of the Plains Indians became a useful craft for
members of the Lewis and Clark expedition on several occasions.
This replica graces the exhibit at the Museum of
Westward Expansion in St. Louis.

men could have carried it over portages, and it would have carried both
passengers and provisions.

As they began to load the craft, a storm blew up. High winds and cold
water battered the boat for hours causing the caulking to peel off the hair-
less skins and leaving the seams exposed. Water filled the boat and it sank.
Lewis speculated that had he left the hair on the hides, the caulking might
have adhered better, but it was too late to try again.

Greatly disappointed, Lewis abandoned the *Experiment* above the
Great Falls, writing on July 9, 1805, "I therefore relinquished all further
hope of my favorite boat."[30] The experimental craft had been designed
to carry four tons of gear. When it didn't work, they were forced to build
two more dugout canoes to haul the necessary gear. They had to leave behind in caches much of their provisions because even with the new canoes,
there was not enough room or carrying capacity. As a result, they ran short
of trade goods and food on the lower Columbia.

SKIN BOATS. On the return trip, Lewis and Clark split the party into two
groups at Traveler's Rest. Lewis took one group by a shortcut to the top of

the Great Falls of the Missouri (the upper end of the portage). When Lewis and his selected men reached the White Bear Islands above the Great Falls, they were on the wrong side of the river. To cross, they killed eleven buffalo and built two skin boats: "one, after the mandan fassion with a single skin in the form of a bason [bullboat] and the other we constructed of two skins on a plan of our own."[31] The next day they transported their baggage and meat to the opposite shore.

While the Indian design called a bullboat might not have seemed a very serviceable craft, it proved more river-worthy then the party of Americans had realized. It took little time to build, and it did the job.

Meanwhile, Clark had led a third of the party from the Three Forks to the Yellowstone on horseback. There, members of his group built the catamaran and headed down the Yellowstone. He left Sergeant Pryor and three men (Hugh Hall, George Shannon, and Richard Windsor) to drive the remainder of the horse herd, twenty-five animals, overland to give to Hugh Heney at the Mandan villages as payment for Heney's pacifying the Teton Sioux. A few nights before Clark headed downstream in the double canoes, the horse herd of forty-nine animals had been cut roughly in half by the theft of twenty-four, presumably by the Crow Indians. On the Pryor party's second night out, the Indians returned to steal the remaining herd, leaving the four men to their collective fate.

Being resourceful, the men returned to the Yellowstone near Pompey's Pillar, killed two buffalo, and using willow wands to make frames, built a pair of bullboats, covering them with the green buffalo hides. They drifted down the Yellowstone to the Missouri, making many miles each day, then followed the Missouri downstream until they caught up with Clark and his party on August 8, 1806, to complete the longest bullboat trip in the expedition's experience.

LOG RAFTS. The hunters frequently had to swim streams or raft them, such as on June 2, 1804: "George Drewyer (Drouillard) and John Shields . . . were obliged to raft or Swim many Creeks."[32] Twice, small parties used log rafts but found them hard to steer; rafts also allowed whatever they carried to get wet. At the mouth of the Marias River, the party faced a major decision: whether the north fork (Marias) or south fork (Missouri) was the true Missouri and the best route.

Lewis explored the Marias River, traveling over a rise of land to get a good perspective of the surrounding country. On his return to the Missouri, he tried to save time by lashing several logs together to form rafts and floating downstream to the camp at the confluence of the Marias with the Missouri. On June 6, 1805, his journal entry reads, "embarcked with our plunder and five Elk's skins on the raft but were soon convinced that this mode of navigation was hazardous particularly with those rafts they being too small and slender. . . . I therefore determined to abandon the rafts and return as we had come, by land."[33]

On the return trip, when Lewis led his party from Traveler's Rest overland to the head of the Great Falls, he crossed Clark Fork River near its confluence with the Bitterroot, using three log rafts (see chapter 7, page 142). On the final of a series of crossings, Lewis was swept off the raft; he floundered ashore, and helped the two nonswimmers in the party land the raft some distance downstream. In the multiple crossings, the log rafts had drifted one and a half miles downstream with the strong current, but all the men and baggage crossed safely.

The Corps of Discovery traveled by water for more than nine thousand miles of the total distance they covered. They used a variety of river craft from keelboat to bullboat, building most of them from natural materials as they moved across the continent. They used basic tools and past experience, adapting Native American ways and their own ingenuity. They made masts, sprits, oars, paddles, poles, and towlines, all from natural materials—one reason archaeologists have found so little evidence of their passage.

Chapter 5

THE RIVERS THEY TRAVELED

Most people who have read their history are aware that Lewis and Clark led an expedition up the Missouri River. Most people know that they also traveled down the Columbia River, but few who haven't read the expedition journals know about their experiences on the Jefferson, Beaverhead, Snake, Clearwater, and Yellowstone.

People often forget about the 1,126-mile trip down the Ohio River and the 184-mile battle against the powerful Mississippi currents the fall of 1803. These voyages positioned the expedition for its attack on the Missouri the following spring. The captains collected many members of the permanent party during their Ohio River cruise, and they began to hone the men's river skills as they worked their way up the Father of Waters.

RIVERS EAST OF THE CONTINENTAL DIVIDE

The Mississippi River and its two major tributaries, the Ohio and the Missouri, drain the vast middle of the United States from Montana to Pennsylvania, from Minnesota and Wisconsin to Texas and the Gulf of Mexico. Dozens of tributaries, large and small, add to the Mississippi and its many branches, augmenting its massive flow. It is well named the Father of Waters; it drains roughly two-thirds of the contiguous forty-eight states, all or parts of thirty-one states.

As noted, the Lewis and Clark expedition began in Pittsburgh where the Monongahela and Allegheny Rivers meet to form the Ohio, where the keelboat was built, and where Lewis began keeping his journal. They traveled more than a thousand miles down the Ohio, gathering expedition members and river experience while hauling gear and provisions to the expedition's base camp near St. Louis. The Ohio River constituted the first leg of the voyage.

The Ohio was well known at the time, had been for decades. George Rogers Clark, the older brother of William Clark, is reported to have built a keelboat (more likely four flatboats) at Pittsburgh in 1778 to haul his troops and supplies down the Ohio during the Revolutionary War. The Ohio and Mississippi Rivers provided the major water route to New Orleans and the open sea by way of the Gulf of Mexico.

More than three hundred keelboats were traveling the Ohio, Mississippi, and Missouri Rivers by 1810. On March 17, 1811, less than five years after the Lewis and Clark expedition returned to St. Louis, the hull of the first steamboat on western waters was launched on the Monongahela River near Pittsburgh.

When the first edition of Zadok Cramer's *The Navigator* was published in 1801 as a guide to the Allegheny, Monongahela, Ohio, and Mississippi Rivers, copies sold for a dollar. The 1808 edition included data from the Lewis and Clark expedition. Cramer revised it almost every year until his death in 1813; his publisher produced new editions through 1824. *The Navigator* not only advised readers about shoals, supply points, landings, and dangers along the rivers but also told its readers where and how to buy boats. In the early days keelboats sold for one dollar a foot, thus forty dollars for a forty-foot boat, and fifty-five dollars for a fifty-five-footer (the Lewis and Clark keelboat cost considerably more).

The Ohio River

Cramer reported that the beauty of the Ohio River begins at the confluence of its creating tributaries. From Pittsburgh it flows thirty miles northwest, then turns to the west of southwest for five hundred miles, then southwest for 160 miles, west for 276 miles, and finally southwest again for another 160 miles, ultimately flowing into the Mississippi some eleven hundred miles below Pittsburgh (Cramer's figures total 1,126 miles, but the distance is often given as a round figure of a thousand miles).

Small river towns embrace the first few miles of the Ohio, the stretch on which Lewis and his crew "were obliged to get out all hands and lift the

[keel]boat over about thirty yards"[1] at *McKee's rock* due to low water. The next day at "big-horse tale riffle" they "wer obliged to unload all our goods and lift the emty Boat over."[2] Later the same day at "Woollery's trap," after unloading again, they hired a team of oxen to move the keelboat through the shallow riffle. For several days they had serious navigation problems that required Lewis to hire horses or oxen to move the keelboat down the river.

Lewis referred to Little Horsetail and Big Horsetail rapids as "ripples." Zadok Cramer used the term as well. Lewis probably meant riffle, *a small rapid with shallow water and waves, a term that the rivermen would have used. A week or so into the trip down the Ohio, Lewis began to use* riffle *instead of* ripple. *My guess is that he simply misheard the term and used* ripple, *which made sense to him, instead of the more common term* riffle *used by the hired pilot. It is possible that during that era, the terms were used interchangeably.*

Below that bend to the southwest at Rochester, Pennsylvania, thirty miles from Pittsburgh, the Ohio River enters West Virginia, which was part of Virginia when Lewis passed through on the keelboat (it become West Virginia during the middle of the Civil War sixty years later). On September 7, their eighth day on the river, they reached Wheeling, where they spent two days, bought a pirogue, and hired a man to work it. Squirrels swimming the river and passenger pigeons migrating south marked the next week. For dinner Lewis ate squirrels his dog Seaman caught in the river.

They began to make good mileage below Wheeling as they found more water and some current: twenty-four, twenty-six, twenty, eighteen miles a day on stretches now marred by dams and locks. They stopped at Marietta, Ohio; spent nearly a week in Cincinnati; picked up Clark and several "young men from Kentucky" in Clarksville, Indiana Territory, at the Falls of the Ohio, which marked the river between Clark's home and Louisville, Kentucky.

On the Ohio, as mentioned in chapter 1, Lewis learned an important lesson about river travel. After "the wind had blown extreemly hard up the river all day," he observed that "the wind on this river . . . blows or sets up agains it's courent [that is, blows upstream] four days out of five during the course of the whole year" and "the wind so frequently sets up the river the way the traveler makes in descending therefore is by dint of hard rowing—or force of the oar or pole."[3] He had discovered that upstream wind patterns dominate most rivers during daylight hours.

After descending "Letart's falls," a rapid with a four-foot drop in 250 yards, on September 18, Lewis stopped writing until November 11, when they reached Fort Massac, a military base on the north (Illinois) side of the river. Here they stayed for two days and recruited George Drouillard as interpreter. Clark wrote his first journal entry November 13, 1803, as the party left Fort "Masacre."[4] The party grew as it traveled down the Ohio. On November 14, they reached the confluence of the Ohio and Mississippi, where they turned upstream and for the first time felt the power of a mighty river moving against the boats that would take them up the Missouri, carrying a heavy load of gear and provisions.

The Mississippi River

Casual readers of the Lewis and Clark story may miss the fact that the expedition traveled up the Mississippi. The mouth of the Ohio is below St. Louis and the mouth of the Missouri. Not only did they power 184 miles up the river to reach their base camp and winter quarters on the Wood River, but they camped near enough to the Mississippi for more than five months, traveling across it on a regular basis back and forth to St. Louis. By the spring of 1804 they had became fairly familiar with the Father of Waters.

Their initial voyage up that powerful river in the fall of 1803 taught the expedition leaders a great deal. The captains soon realized they needed more men to power their crafts against the strong currents of these heartland rivers. They doubled the number of permanent party members and recruited additional crew to man the pirogues.

During their time on the Mississippi, November 20 to December 12, they averaged only eight miles a day. At the mouth of the Ohio they encountered numerous sandbars, typical of major river junctures. Both rivers carry great quantities of sand and silt, which tend to settle in the conflicting currents battling for control at their confluence. The expedition experienced the same pattern at the mouth of the Platte River.

The slow-moving Ohio meets the Mississippi in a relatively flat landscape; wherever the current slows, sand and silt settle out, and sandbars and islands form. Since conflicting confluence currents constantly change speed, direction, and volume, the islands and sandbars often alter from day to day, even hour to hour, as Mark Twain pointed out much later in *Life on the Mississippi*, still a good book to read to understand what the Corps of Discovery was facing.

Lewis observed, "The Mississippi when full throws large quantitys of mud into the mouths of these [tributary] rivers whose courents not being equal to contend with it's power become still or eddy for many miles up them."[5] He explains that because the main river is so powerful and most tributaries so short and relatively powerless, they must flow through the mud flats left by the Mississippi to make their presence known. In effect, the more powerful river dams the weaker, slowing their currents enough to allow silt and sand to settle in their mouths, choking them until their own currents cut a way through the silt when the level of the larger river drops.

As the expedition moved upstream, Lewis found the "current rapid and difficult" and "the iner part of every bend . . . is always filled with Islands."[6] Again, this is typical of most rivers: the stronger faster current on the outside of the bends deepens the channel and keeps the sand and silt from settling. Instead, it settles on the inside of the bends where the current slows, forming islands and sandbars, another lesson learned by the fledgling river explorers. At river mouths in flat terrain, sand and silt form islands.

Despite their slow rate of travel, they "overtook two keels [keelboats] from Louisville bound to Kaskaskias loaded with dry goods and whiskey,"[7] evidence of traffic on the river. Their upstream travel may have been slow—ten miles in eight and a half hours on November 24, ten miles in nine and a half hours on November 26—but after November 28, when Clark took command of the flotilla, the expedition began making better mileage: fourteen and three-quarter miles the first day in ten and a half hours, nineteen and one-quarter miles a few days later in a little more than nine hours, then ten and three-quarter miles in less than five and a half hours, and thirteen and a half miles in seven and a half hours, a noticeable difference. Perhaps the better mileage reflected slower current; perhaps the men were learning to manage the boats better; perhaps they had a good tail wind; or perhaps Clark was simply a better riverman.

They reached Wood River at 2 P.M. on December 12, in a storm against a strong northwest wind. They had traveled eleven and one-quarter miles in six and one-quarter hours, almost two miles an hour, one of their faster days as they moved the boats against the powerful currents of the Mississippi. The hunters who were sent out to supply dinner found only turkeys and opossum; such was their first meal at Camp Dubois, their base camp and winter home.

Shortly after landing to camp in the rain, the men saw two canoes full of Potawatomi Indians land nearby, having crossed the mighty river through wind and waves that should have swamped them. Clark noted that "they were all Drunk and their Canoo had not received any water,"[8] the expedition's first example of Native American canoeing prowess.

The Missouri River

In his 1945 book, *The Missouri*, Stanley Vestal wrote that the Missouri River "was not only the main highway to the West, it was also the base of operations for the winning of the West."[9] Calling it "a thoroughly masculine river, a burley, husky bulldozer of a stream," Vestal saw the Missouri as "a highway that . . . has captured the imagination of mankind,"[10] echoing Nebraska poet John Neihardt.

To Neihardt, it was "the river of an unwritten epic." Best known for his interpretation of Lakota holy man Black Elk's vision quest in *Black Elk Speaks*, Nebraskan Neihardt found the muddy Missouri River irresistible. In 1908 he canoed two thousand miles of the unfettered Missouri and wrote a book about his experience called *The River and I*, still in print nearly a century after it first appeared (1910). In this book he writes, "I am more thrilled by the history of the Lewis and Clark expedition than [by] the tale of Jason."[11]

Like members of the expedition, he saw the Great Falls before they were dammed, their waters diverted for more practical purposes. His pictures of the falls, taken a century after Lewis and Clark saw them and Lewis wrote so glowingly about them, appear in his book. We shall never again see the falls as expedition members experienced them. They are gone as surely as Celilo Falls on the Columbia.

The Corps of Discovery traveled up the Missouri during the spring, summer, and fall of 1804, averaging fewer than ten miles a day. They knew the general course of the Missouri, knew that by following it upstream they would reach the Mandan country, even knew that the Mandan were friendly traders and farmers and could supply them with food.

The Missouri was well known and well traveled. Two or three times a week the men of the expedition met people in canoes or pirogues heading downriver to St. Louis with furs, hides, bear oil, buffalo tallow, ginseng, and other products of the plains through which the river coursed. The area was once home to the Missouri, Pawnee, and Kaw (Kansas); the Oto, Osage, and Omaha; the Ioway, Sioux, and Cheyenne; the Arikara and Mandan—a vast land that today comprises the states of Missouri, Kansas, Iowa, Nebraska, and the Dakotas.

In the fall of 2001, Rod Nash and I canoed twenty-seven miles of the middle Missouri from the base of Fort Randall Dam to the mouth of the Choteau River several miles above Running Water, South Dakota, near the mouth of the Niobrara River on the Nebraska side (there aren't many roads in the area). The segment Nash and I paddled— wide and shallow with a backdrop of rolling hills, many cut by the river—includes the stretch that George Shannon traveled when he was lost for two weeks. Today the adjacent land is either private ranchland or Indian reservation.

We camped not far from the prairie dog town that the expedition visited. Trying to dig out or drown out the curious creatures, they captured one and ate it for supper. In this vicinity, through which they passed in early September, 1804, they saw their first pronghorn, their first mule deer, and Lewis killed a buffalo in the river. Buffalo and wolves were abundant. We saw no buffalo, pronghorn, or wolves, but we did see osprey and bald eagles, great blue heron and kingfishers, ducks and geese, and cormorants.

After wintering with the Mandan in what would become North Dakota, they continued up the Missouri in the spring of 1805, sending the keelboat back to St. Louis because the river had become too shallow to float the big craft. They used the two pirogues and six dugout canoes they had built near Fort Mandan during the winter.

Before long they reached the mouth of the Yellowstone, recognized it

Citadel Rock on the Upper Missouri was noted by William Clark
in his journal on May 31, 1805.

as a significant river, and decided to explore it on their return. They encountered wildlife in such abundance that they lived high on the hog,
killing much more meat than they could possibly consume. As they moved
westward, they entered the Missouri River Breaks and the White Cliffs
area, which impressed them. Lewis waxed eloquent in his journal entry
(May 31, 1805) about the formations that "exhibit a most romantic appearance."[12]

Above the White Cliffs area the men became puzzled when they came
to the confluence of what they named Maria's River. Was it or was the left
fork the true Missouri? They spent a week exploring both and went up the
left fork, which was indeed the true Missouri, for they soon came to the
Great Falls.

They cached both pirogues before reaching the Great Falls; the canoes
they portaged around the falls, an eighteen-mile detour that took them almost a month. Above the falls, as mentioned earlier, they built two more
canoes to haul gear the iron boat had been designed to carry.

Up the Missouri they went, passing through the Gates of the Mountains and stopping at the Three Forks to decide which one to take and to
name them: Gallatin, Madison, and Jefferson. They followed the latter,

The Missouri River Breaks, now a national monument, also has the
protection of National Wild and Scenic River status.

named for the president of the United States who had sent them on this
expedition. It too forked, and they made another decision at the confluence of the Big Hole and Beaverhead. After some confusion, they followed the latter to still another fork, where they left the river, sinking their
canoes in a nearby pond to protect and preserve them for the return trip,
and traveled overland by horseback.

This final fork has today been inundated by a reservoir. The true source
of the Missouri is generally accepted as being the Red Rock River flowing out of Red Rock Lakes a few miles west of Yellowstone National Park
from the slopes of Mount Jefferson. The fork the expedition followed
overland to Lemhi Pass is Horse Prairie Creek, which lies more than three
thousand miles from the mouth of the Missouri.

Taken together, the Missouri-Mississippi River is the world's second
longest after Africa's Nile. The Missouri itself ranks as the longest river on
the North American continent. From its headwaters at Red Rock Lakes,
now a national wildlife refuge where trumpeter swans nest and mosquitoes thrive, it passes through a constantly changing landscape. Its pristine
wetlands serve as habitat for ducks, geese, shorebirds, numerous forest

The Marias River flows into the Missouri River from the left, below
the island in the foreground, at this famous confluence where the
Lewis and Clark expedition camped for nearly a week
while trying to determine which fork was the true Missouri.

species, abundant raptors, and the largest population of mountain blue-
birds I have ever seen.

These headwater trout streams, flowing out of high-elevation marshes
rarely visited by tourists in nearby Yellowstone and Grand Teton national
parks, were never seen by expedition members, but they may well repre-
sent a landscape more similar to the one they found than that of the well-
traveled modern tourism routes. The landscape offers the kinds of vistas,
isolation, and solitude that the Corps of Discovery came to know so well
and to enjoy and appreciate. Such places, common to Lewis and Clark, are
rare today and rapidly disappearing.

The Missouri has been dammed and polluted, its waters diverted
for irrigation and power production. The Great Falls of the Missouri
no longer roar; dams lie above all of its major drops. Its flow through the
Gates of the Mountains has been stilled by another dam and caught in a
series of reservoirs.

In *Paddling Montana*, the Fischers, old acquaintances, tell about the
dams: "In Montana, nearly a third of the Missouri lies stilled behind concrete and earth. First come Canyon Ferry, Hauser, and Holter dams, three
dams in succession that lie east of Helena and impound the river for nearly
70 miles. Then near downtown Great Falls lie five run-of-the-river dams
that check the famous falls where Lewis and Clark made an arduous 17-
mile portage."[13]

These all lie below the Three Forks of the Missouri. The dam on the Beaverhead inundates its creating confluence with Horse Prairie Creek; its reservoir is named for Clark. Another dam upstream impounds Red Rock River. Fort Peck Dam in eastern Montana drowns nearly one hundred miles of the Missouri, creating one of the world's largest reservoirs.

In the name of dubious flood control, the Missouri has been dammed, diked, and dredged, channelized and tamed, turned into corporate welfare tax shelters and barge boondoggles: dams that subsidize the barge industry and agribusiness at the expense of Indian tribes, recreational boating and fishing, fish and wildlife including several endangered species such as the pallid sturgeon, the interior least tern, and the piping plover. It is currently a hot political issue in the Dakotas, Iowa, and Nebraska, testing whether the Army Corps of Engineers should listen to the taxpaying public or to the special interests that benefit from their works. The American taxpayers foot the bills.

Six major dams lie below the 149-mile Wild and Scenic River stretch: Fort Peck Dam and reservoir, Garrison Dam and "Lake" Sakakawea, Oahe Dam and "Lake," Big Bend Dam and reservoir, Fort Randall Dam, and Gavins Point Dam, all on the middle Missouri between Great Falls, Montana, and Sioux City, Iowa.

Below Sioux City, the river is designed for barge traffic. The Corps of Engineers has built wing dams to force the current into the center of the river to deepen the channel "naturally," but these rocky protrusions create dangerous eddies for human-powered crafts and small power boats. The lower Missouri has been altered beyond recognition. Major efforts are now under way in several states to curb the Army Corps of Engineers and return the Missouri to a more natural state.

THE THREE FORKS. The Missouri River actually begins at the Three Forks, the Jefferson, Madison, and Gallatin northwest of present-day Bozeman in central Montana. During spring snowmelt when it floods, it is often difficult to differentiate one fork from another, for they form one broad slowly moving wetland. The Gallatin, most easterly of the three forks, enters the main river well below the confluence of the Madison and Jefferson forks where the Missouri River officially originates

Each fork braids and meanders, forming a network of channels to confuse the eye as it spreads over a mile of riparian habitat, drowning beaver ponds and destroying their dams and lodges. Fishing is lousy and boating

The Three Forks of the Missouri confirmed the fact that the
expedition was on the right route to the Shoshone. Lewis and Clark
named the rivers for President Thomas Jefferson, Secretary of State
James Madison, and Secretary of Treasury Albert Gallatin.

is dangerous during high water, but much of the year all three forks flow
clear and mellow, offering good fishing and fine boating.

The Three Forks all offer exciting river running possibilities: the East
Fork of the Gallatin runs through Bozeman; the West Fork drains the Big
Sky Ski Resort. Clark's overland route to the Yellowstone River in the
summer of 1806 followed the Gallatin. In the summer of 1995, Dave
Green and I rafted its whitewater from the North Fork; we encountered
difficult Class V rapids during spring runoff, the water high, fast, and cold.

The Madison, which forms at the junction of the Firehole and Gibbon
Rivers in Yellowstone National Park, is dammed three times, twice by
human-made structures and once by a natural landslide caused by an
earthquake, which I experienced in the summer of 1959. It includes the
remote Bear Trap Canyon, full of rattlesnakes, great fishing, and serious
rapids that only the expert rafter or kayaker should attempt.

From the Three Forks, the Missouri flows northward, initially northwest, then northeast. Following it upstream in the opposite direction the

late summer of 1805, the expedition worried about its turn to the south, especially when it curved east of south above the mouth of the Dearborn. It seemed to be taking them in the wrong direction. It was a roundabout route, but had they not followed it, they would not have found the Shoshone Indians from whom they obtained the horses they needed to cross the Continental Divide.

Below the Great Falls, the Missouri continues flowing northeast. Shortly after the Marias River joins it, the Missouri makes a big loop southward, then turns more easterly, flowing through a designated 149-mile Wild and Scenic Rivers stretch, recently given national monument status as well. The protected section includes the White Cliffs and the badlands of the Missouri Breaks. Then it passes through the Charles M. Russell National Wildlife Refuge and into Fort Peck Reservoir.

The summers of 2002 and 2003, I canoed sixty miles of the upper Missouri from Coal Bank Landing to the McClelland Ferry several miles below the mouth of the Judith River, which Clark named for the woman he married (Lewis wanted to call it the Bighorn). The Missouri was muddy; the Judith, even muddier. I found a four-pound catfish on a trotline anchored at the mouth of the Judith, a clear stream when the expedition passed.

On this stretch of the Missouri I found both limber pine and box elder where Lewis first described them, three rattlesnakes, and plenty of beaver sign. I experienced two tremendous thunderstorms, saw the "points of rocks" that so frustrated the men towing the pirogues and canoes through this stretch. One evening I heard a coyote chorus. I felt I was traveling in the expedition's footsteps. All this the expedition experienced when the area was truly wild.

From a high elevation in the Badlands on May 26, 1805, Clark wrote, "from this point I beheld the Rocky Mountains for the first time with Certainty."[14] From the same point I saw distant snow peaks. Later, Lewis wrote, "The hills and river Clifts which we passed today exhibit a most romantic appearance. The bluffs of the river rise to the height of from 2 to 300 feet and in most places nearly perpendicular; they are formed of remarkable white sandstone which is sufficiently soft to give way readily to the impression of water."[15]

He was much impressed and wrote further about "clifts ... woarn ... into a thousand grotesque figures" and "parapets well stocked with statuary," of "collumns of various sculpture both grooved and plain . . . supporting long galleries," and of "pedestals and capitals." Most of them remain for us to see today; I saw them the summers of 2002 and 2003.

THE JEFFERSON RIVER. From Twin Bridges, Montana, the Jefferson Fork of the Missouri flows northeast through the heart of western Montana: Silver Star, Waterloo, Parsons Bridge, Whitehall; then it turns more easterly past Kountz Bridge and Mayflower Bridge, Cardwell and LaHood Park, Drouillard, and on to the Three Forks. Modern Montana highways 41 and 55 and U.S. 287 follow it.

This sixty-mile segment, flanked by the Tobacco Root Mountains to the east and the Highland Mountains to the west, gave the expedition some of its toughest going upstream: swift current, shallow water, the shores heavy with willows, and beaver ponds flanking the route, frustrating attempts to tow the canoes. There was no easy tow path. Now largely cattle country, the Jefferson can be floated, although logjams, protruding trees (sweepers), narrow channels, and swift water offer the same hazards the Corps of Discovery came to know. Diversion dams add a modern hazard the expedition did not experience. Fishing for brown trout, an introduced species, can be good. Moose enjoy the adjacent marshy habitat and beaver still abound.

Below the Forks of the Jefferson (the confluence of the Big Hole with the Beaverhead and the beginning of today's Jefferson River), Clark wrote on August 4, 1805, that the forks were "crouded with Islands Sholey rapid & clear," and that the men had to "haul the Canoes over the rapids, which Succeed each other every two or three hundred yards and between the water rapid oblige to towe & walke on Stones the whole day except when we have poleing men wet all day Sore feet."[16]

Clark started the canoes up the Big Hole. Lewis had left a note telling them to take the left fork, but he posted it on a green pole, which the beavers cut, and the note was lost. Drouillard found them and told them of their mistake. Turning the heavy dugouts around in the rapid water to retreat down the Big Hole, they swamped two canoes, capsized another, and had a difficult time reversing their course. Whitehouse was almost killed. Lewis, who did not witness the accident, wrote on August 6, 1805, that, "Whitehouse had been thrown out of one of the canoes as she swing in a rapid current and the canoe had rubed him and pressed him to the bottom as she passed over him and had the water been 2 inches shallower must inevitably have crushed him to death."[17]

During the summer of 1995, Dave Green and I found the confluence much as Clark had described it. Locating a launch site a few miles up the Big Hole, which both captains called "the rapid fork," we decided that even at flood stage, we could handle the river and run the section that had given the expedition so much trouble. Faster than the Beaverhead but wider, more open, the Big Hole at high water seemed easier than Lewis and Clark had described it.

Dave and I enjoyed the whitewater, but we had all that we could handle when we reached the confluence with the Beaverhead. The rivers roared through a series of flooded cottonwood-covered islands that disintegrated before our eyes as undercut trees swept into the current, threatening to capsize our canoe. We bobbed about like porpoises, sawyers thrashing, trees blocking channels, a descent to the maelstrom.

We ran two or three miles in twenty minutes, fearing for our lives every second as we swept through the chaos. Now we were on the Jefferson, a broad swift river with higher banks and no islands. The river still flooded lowlands, rose into the riverside shrubbery, lapped at the base of trees. It still carried flood debris, whole trees and driftwood, but it was manageable now. Once again we felt in control, as we had not during our passage through the confluence. Then we saw my parked pick-up, our take out. I was happy to have safely negotiated that chaotic confusing confluence, but now I hated to leave the river

The Beaverhead River

The Beaverhead takes its name from Beaverhead Rock north of Dillon, Montana, a formation that Sacagawea recognized as a feature of her homeland, encouraging news to the expedition leaders because they knew they were on the right route to the Shoshone. Today it is a clear, swift-flowing stream popular with fly fishermen. Flowing with reservoir release water, it was the only canoeable river we found in southwestern Montana in late June of 1995. All the others were flooding with snowmelt runoff.

Green and I had come to explore Lewis and Clark rivers when days were longest. Seeing the Beaverhead about 4 P.M., we decided to run a short stretch before dark. I left Dave and my canoe at the highway cross-

When Sacagawea recognized Beaverhead Rock, the river's
namesake, Lewis and Clark knew they had reached the country of
the Shoshone Indians, Sacagawea's people, who had horses.

ing near Beaverhead Rock, drove the twelve miles to a park at the edge
of Twin Bridges, Montana, where I left my pick-up truck and hitch-hiked
back to our launch site (the first car to drive by gave me a lift). The afternoon was warm and sunny.

We hit the river at 5 P.M., found it fast but negotiable, full of bends and
riffles but no rapids. The willow-covered bank provided an intimate experience and also cover for wildlife, from fox, deer, and beaver, to birds of
every size, shape, and color: white pelicans, great blue herons, red-winged
and yellow-headed blackbirds, a ring-necked pheasant, and even a great
horned owl as dusk set in.

The river meanders so severely that at one point we could see across
three oxbows, a discouraging perspective for the Corps of Discovery towing, poling, and manhandling the heavy canoes as they traveled upstream.
But we were traveling downstream, going with the current.

Paddling hard to reach our destination before dark, we stopped for
nothing; we must have been moving at least five miles an hour, but as the
day drew to a close, we had not yet reached Ruby River (the expedition's
Philanthropy), a good way above Twin Bridges. Only later, when we con-
sulted accurate maps, did we realize the distance by river was twenty-six

miles, more than twice the highway mileage. By the time we reached our take-out, we had been paddling in the dark for an hour.

At the beginning of the Beaverhead, the expedition left the river to travel overland by horseback. On their return the following spring, part of the Corps of Discovery once more took to the river at the same point they had left it, followed the Beaverhead to the Jefferson, the Jefferson to the Three Forks, then floated the Missouri to the Great Falls, and performed the portage once more. The entire party reunited on the Missouri and headed for St. Louis.

Despite the constant hard work on the river, their illness and indisposition, their frustration in dealing with local inhabitants, their worries about the weather, their route, and their slow progress, the captains could enjoy the beauty of the land through which they traveled. They had a job to do, and they did it, following the Missouri to its head of navigation. It led them to grand discoveries. It remains a glorious river despite its dams and floodplain development and the decimation of its wildlife and native people who lived along its banks.

RIVERS WEST OF THE CONTINENTAL DIVIDE

West of the Continental Divide, Lewis and Clark found a confusing jumble of mountains and a complex network of streams, a discouraging perspective, given their primary goal. They had anticipated a single river flowing directly west to the Pacific. They found rivers, but they didn't seem to go where the explorers wanted to go. Some, like the Salmon River, now a popular attraction for recreational river runners, were too rambunctious for safe travel. Others were beset with serious but negotiable rapids, with terrifying falls they were forced to portage. Finding any water route to the Pacific would not be easy.

All of the rivers flowing westward produced prodigious numbers of salmon and steelhead as well as sturgeon and other fish that kept the expedition from starving. All of them led to the Pacific Ocean, their goal, but none of them led as directly to the ocean as they had hoped. Some rivers flowed through arid country devoid of trees, a basaltic landscape that offered formidable barriers to river travel.

The rivers the Corps of Discovery knew back home in the eastern United States were tame compared to these western rivers. In more than

At Canoe Camp on the Clearwater River, immediately across from
the mouth of its North Fork, the expedition built five more
dugout canoes, using fire to burn out the hollows.

three thousand miles, the Missouri had climbed only twenty-eight hundred feet, an average of less than a foot a mile. In the 640-mile course down
the Clearwater, Snake, and Columbia, the rivers dropped more than sixteen hundred feet, an average of two and a half feet per mile. It was a faster
river system carved through a basaltic block of much harder bedrock than
the expedition had yet experienced. West of the Divide they found a different world, both on the river and off.

The Clearwater River

When the Lewis and Clark expedition stumbled out of the Bitterroot
Mountains in the fall of 1805, they found themselves on the Clearwater
River in Nez Perce country. The Nez Perce called it the Kooskooskee. On
the banks of this clear-water river opposite its North Fork the expedition
built canoes, as mentioned before, using fire for the first time to hollow out
their dugouts, following a technique they learned from the Nez Perce.

The Clearwater begins at the confluence of the Lochsa and Selway
Rivers in central Idaho, flowing from a network of streams that head in the
Selway-Bitterroot Wilderness, their courses protected by the National
Wild and Scenic Rivers System. The Clearwater and its Selway source

were among the original "instant-eight" wild rivers protected when the act became law in October, 1968.

———~———

Traveling with wilderness historian Roderick Nash and one of his former students, Taz Talley, I ran the Selway the summer of 1981, the highlight of my river-running career: it was the most challenging river I had ever negotiated. The entire forty-seven-mile-wild segment courses through true wilderness only a few miles from the Lewis and Clark route. Seeing elk, black bear, mule deer, bighorn sheep, coyotes, bald eagles, and a mountain lion on the drive to the launch site, we might have been with Lewis and Clark. We discussed wilderness against the background of the expedition's experience, comparing it to our own river adventure.

The Selway was cold, clear, swift, and unknown; none of us had run it before. We knew little more about the Selway River than Lewis and Clark had known about the Clearwater when they launched onto its waters in the fall of 1805. Our rafts swept down the steep river, an average drop of twenty-eight feet per mile, more than ten times the drop of the Clearwater itself, so fast we had little time to think. We just reacted to keep the rafts in the current, off the rocks, out of the holes.

Like the Corps of Discovery, we weren't always successful. We hit holes and shipped waves, filling our boats with cold water. We read the river and rowed, dodging rocks and haystacks, setting up for a series of increasingly more difficult rapids. By the time we reached our first campsite at Running Creek, we were all wet, cold, exhausted—as the members of the Lewis and Clark expedition were nearly every day.

Hiking the hills above camp the next morning, we saw a bear that Rod swears was a grizzly—he got a better look at it than I did—and we thought again of Lewis and Clark. Below Moose Creek, rapids got bigger with the increased volume, a series of five major drops in seven miles. We spent the afternoon hiking the trail on the right bank, scouting the rapids, making sketches, taking notes, as Lewis and Clark would have.

After breakfast the next day, our nervous party launched early. The rapids blurred together. We ran two before I realized we'd reached the first one. All our markers had disappeared. We caught an eddy and landed to scout the next several rapids again to reorient ourselves.

The rapids came too quickly, too close together to stop; we ran the next three before we could catch an eddy. With heavy canoes in fast water, the Corps of Discovery often had trouble stopping. They hit rocks, split canoes, took on water; canoes lodged on midriver rocks or sank in the swift current. We hit rocks and took on water, but we split no canoes—we were rowing rubber rafts. We were pioneers on that trip through the Selway-Bitterroot wilderness; we felt akin to Lewis and Clark, who had passed nearby on their overland trip along Clark's (the Bitterroot) River, which we had crossed several times on our drive to the launch site. We traveled similar territory.

The Selway provides water to the Clearwater, but when Lewis and Clark started down the Clearwater in the fall of 1805, they had relatively little water. The river was low on October 6, the day they finished building the canoes. Clark reported a cold wind off the mountains, "untill the Suns gets to Some hight" and the river "is Clear rapid with Shoals or Swift places,"[18] evidence of the ways of wind and water: the normal daily nocturnal-diurnal wind patterns and autumn low water in the river with lots of rocks showing and the channels narrow.

The next day they loaded the canoes and launched. They ran into trouble almost immediately. They "proced on passd maney bad rapids."[19] Clark's canoe struck a rock and sprung a leak in the third rapid. They ran ten rapids, made twenty miles, and repaired the canoe overnight. The second day, Gass's canoe hit a rock, split, and sank. The third day they spent repairing canoes and drying goods wet in the accident. On the fourth day they reached the Snake, having covered sixty miles in three days of actual time on the river. The Snake's "greenish blue" color contrasted with the Clearwater's pellucidity.

When the party reached the Clearwater on their eastward trek, they were delayed for nearly a month, waiting for the snow to melt in the Bitterroot passes. To ferry hunters and food purchased from the Nez Perce Indians across the Clearwater on a daily basis, the expedition borrowed canoes from the natives. In May, they built their own, burning it out (May 22–25), finishing it and launching it (May 26) on a fast, rising river, an indication that the snows were melting at last.

But unable to deal with the high, fast water, on May 30, with Shannon and Collins manning the craft, "in landing on the opposite shore the canoe

The Clearwater River courses through the living heart of Nez Perce
Country, a clear fast stream flowing out of steep terrain. It took
the expedition from the mountains to the Snake River.

was driven broad side with the full forse of a very strong current against
some standing trees and instantly filled with water and sunk,"[20] according
to Lewis's journal entry. Potts, a passenger in the canoe and a poor swimmer, barely made the shore.

Ordway reported the men got safely ashore but lost three trade blan-
kets. They thought they had lost the canoe as well, but on June 8, Ordway
reported, "a number of the natives joined and got out our canoe which was
sank."[21] A few days later they left the canoe with the Nez Perce when they
finally departed the Clearwater on horseback to cross the Bitterroots.

The Snake River

The lower Snake River provided the route the Corps of Discovery followed from the Clearwater to the Columbia the fall of 1805. They did not
follow it upstream the spring of 1806; they found traveling against the Columbia's powerful current in the spring flood too time-consuming, difficult, and dangerous. Instead, they traveled overland by horse to the mouth
of the Clearwater, cutting across the Snake's big bend through present-
day southeastern Washington.

From their camp on the Clearwater, in the spring of 1806, they sent a party overland to the Snake (Nez Perce say Salmon) when they learned it was running thick with steelhead before the big sea-run rainbow trout reached the Clearwater. Expedition journalists called them salmon trout.

The party named the Snake after Lewis, but the name never stuck except for a distant tributary that the expedition never saw. For a time the modern Snake was known as the South Fork of Lewis's River; the modern Salmon River, as the East Fork. Lewis River and Lake in southern Yellowstone National Park remain the only bodies of water in the Snake River system that carry the Lewis name today.

The Snake got its name from the Shoshone Indians who lived along its banks. The Indian sign language symbol for this tribe is a waving motion of the hand, thumb up, away from the body. Trappers, thinking it looked like the motion of a snake, called the tribe the Snakes and the river along which they lived, the Snake. Other explanations for the sign suggest the waving motion may have meant that they wove baskets or that they lived along a crooked river or even that they ate fish.

Formed by melting snows and springs along the Continental Divide in southern Yellowstone National Park and the Teton Wilderness, the Snake River flows more than nine hundred miles before the Clearwater enters it at present-day Lewiston, Idaho (across from Clarkston, Washington).

Headwaters drain the Teton and Gros Ventre ranges in northwestern Wyoming; tributaries flow from northern Utah and Nevada, southern Idaho, eastern Oregon, and southeastern Washington. The Snake thus drains parts of six states. It forms the boundary between Idaho and Oregon in Hells Canyon and part of the Idaho-Washington boundary before flowing into the Columbia at the modern Tri-Cities area of Kennewick-Pasco-Richland in the state of Washington. The point between the two rivers is known today as Sacagawea State Park.

The explorers never knew Hells Canyon, though Ordway, as mentioned above, led a small party on horseback to trade for fish at Wild Goose Rapid below Hells Canyon proper (Nez Perce elder Allen Pinkham says it was the Salmon). They found fish and bought seventeen of them, but it took them three days to haul them back to the party encamped on the Clearwater; the fish had spoiled before the men could eat them.

The portion of the Snake that Lewis and Clark traveled westward courses through the basaltic plains of southeastern Washington State, a steep but gently rolling region that the expedition traversed on horseback as they returned to the Clearwater. The river has cut a steep gorge through hard, dark, columnar basalt. Four modern dams have turned this portion of the Snake into a series of impoundments: Lower Granite, Little Goose, Lower Monumental, and Ice Harbor. They have drowned the huge angular blocks and solid bedrock that beset the channel when the Corps of Discovery negotiated its way downstream to the Columbia.

Steep canyon walls limited their camping possibilities, confining them to old Indian camps full of fleas and feces. They found little firewood for cooking and not much to cook except Indian dogs purchased from the fishing tribes who lived along the river. The river flowed fast and furiously through the rocky gorge, too fast for maneuvering the heavy dugout canoes safely through. As usual, they hit rocks, split canoes, took on water, ground to a stop on midriver bedrock, swamped canoes and sank a few, but they powered on through to the Columbia.

The Snake River was merely a means to an end; they paid it little attention except to follow its course to the Columbia. The modern cities of Lewiston, Idaho, and Clarkston, Washington, lie on opposite sides of the Snake at the mouth of the Clearwater. Situated in the deep gorge carved by the rivers through lava flows, these twin cities have become seaports as a result of the four downstream dams on the Snake and the four dams on the Columbia below the Snake's mouth. The entire stretch of Snake River that Lewis and Clark traveled is now flat water, all of its rapids drowned, its voice stilled beneath a string of dying reservoirs. With the stench of pulp mills rather than dead fish dominating the confluence, Lewis and Clark would not recognize it.

The Columbia River

One of the major rivers of the Pacific Northwest, the Columbia drains parts of seven states and one Canadian province to produce 281 million acre feet of annual discharge into the Pacific Ocean, a massive amount of water as the Corps of Discovery learned in the spring of 1806 when they tried to fight their way up the powerful currents generated by spring snowmelt and almost continuous rainfall. The Columbia was once a mighty river by almost anyone's standards, undiscovered by people of European descent until 1792. Now it is largely a string of reservoirs.

Eight hundred miles of the Columbia's 1,450-mile length is no longer a river: it is flat water, impoundment, holding pond, bathtub. The Colum-

Hat Rock, the remnant of a volcanic basaltic plug, today lies in an
Oregon state park. Camped across the Columbia, Clark wrote
(October 19, 1805) of a rock "resembling a hat."

bia is dammed three times in Canada, and eleven times in the United
States. Of its 745-mile length in the United States, only fifty miles above
tidal influence flow freely. Lewis and Clark knew only the lower 350 miles
of the Columbia, but four dams now block the flow of the once mighty Columbia below the mouth of the Snake, where the Corps of Discovery first
encountered it and followed it to the Pacific.

Beginning in a great trench in British Columbia, it flows for two hundred miles northwest, augmented by the Kicking Horse, to run head-on
into the Canoe River, flowing southeast in that same trench, just above the
first dam at Mica Creek near David Thompson's 1811 Boat Encampment.
(Thompson explored the Columbia for Great Britain five years after the
expedition headed home.) Here it turns south toward Canada's border
with the United States, enlarged by the flow of the Canadian Kootenay
(Kootenai in the United States), the Pend Oreille, and the Clark Fork.

In the state of Washington it zigs and zags, accepting the flow of the
Spokane, Methow, Wenatchee, Yakima, and Snake, its largest tributary.
Forty-two percent of the Columbia's drainage system lies in the Snake
River drainage. Below the mouth of the Snake, where Lewis and Clark
first paddled its waters, the Umatilla, John Day, Deschutes, Willamette,
and Cowlitz increase its volume. The Columbia's flow into the Pacific av-

erages 265,000 cubic feet per second, roughly half the flow of the Mississippi's but considerably more than the Yukon's.

———— ∿ ————

I'd driven along the Columbia River Gorge a number of times and had mediated a dispute concerning deep-water port development in the Columbia River estuary at Astoria. I'd rafted the Methow, Wenatchee, John Day, and Deschutes (Columbia tributaries); canoed the Yakima and Cowlitz, but I really became familiar with the Columbia at river level when I traveled from Washougal, Washington, where the expedition camped for nearly a week, to the mouth of the Snake in Roderick Nash's twenty-eight-foot Nordic tugboat Forevergreen, *the guest of my old river-running buddy. We negotiated the locks of four Columbia River dams and stopped at several Lewis and Clark sites, anchoring one night at Rock Creek where the Corps had camped. We spent a couple of hours exploring Miller Island where Lewis and Clark had found an Indian graveyard, the bodies encased in canoes.*

In the fall of 2002 and 2003, I once more familiarized myself with the route the expedition followed, traveling from Portland, Oregon, to Clarkston, Washington, on a Lindblad cruise as a Lewis and Clark historian. We took a side trip by jetboat into Hells Canyon, where I once guided raft trips; we visited the Nez Perce National Historical Park. We then followed the river route downstream to Fort Clatsop near the river's mouth. Nothing compares to being there for understanding the expedition's challenges, even with most of the route dammed.

———— ∿ ————

The Columbia has changed in the nearly two hundred years since the Corps of Discovery followed its channels. Gone are Celilo Falls, inundated by the waters of The Dalles Dam. Gone are the Long and Short Narrows, drowned in the impoundment behind Bonneville Dam. Native American fishermen still take salmon and steelhead in the wide waters of the former river, but Lewis and Clark would have lost their directions as salmon and steelhead now do, given the lack of current in the reservoirs. It would have taken them longer to reach the ocean, but they'd have had an easier upriver trip—except for portaging the dams.

My most intimate experience with the Columbia came during the

spring of 2002 when I canoed a short segment of the lower river with fish-
eries biologist Jack Remington. We launched his canoe at mid-morning
on the lower John Day River (the one near Astoria) and began paddling
against an incoming tide. Once we reached the Columbia, we turned upstream to use the tide, paddling through the islands of Lewis and Clark
National Wildlife Refuge, seeing a variety of birds, from bald eagles and
osprey to great blue heron, Canada geese, and several species of ducks.

We stopped for lunch on a small island, waiting for the tide to turn, then
paddled up a tiny tributary, Bear River according to our chart, and found a
trio of nutria sunning on a log. Serenaded by red-winged blackbirds in the
bordering cattails, we watched pintails feeding in the marsh and coots
dinking in and out of the reeds. In this vicinity, protected by the islands,
the expedition crossed from the north shore to the south, where they wintered on a small tributary near the river's mouth. On these very islands the
members of the expedition hunted deer and waterfowl. We hunted with
them, using our binoculars and our imaginations.

We followed the tide back to the mouth of the John Day near Tongue
Point, site of another expedition camp. Tongue Point has been developed,
the riverbed dredged to deepen it for ocean-going vessels. Some of the islands we saw had not been here when Lewis and Clark came through; they
are dredge-spoil dumps.

An endangered species of terns has colonized one of these human-
made islands. During their nesting season they feed heavily on salmon
and steelhead smolt that are moving toward their ocean pastures. When an
endangered species threatens another endangered species due to human
interference, what should be done? Move the terns? Screen the river?
Barge the smolt to the river's mouth? Every attempt by the human species
to play god seems to complicate or compromise natural systems.

We loaded the canoe on Jack's pick-up and headed down river to look
at replica dugout canoes on the bank of Lewis and Clark River at Fort
Clatsop National Memorial. Here the party wintered: they endured nearly
constant rain; ate roots, dried salmon, and spoiled elk; and occasionally lost
their canoes to the tides. In the spring of 1806 they headed up the Columbia, watching the tides carefully, in three of their old dugout canoes
and three Indian canoes. In the spring of 2003 Jack and I returned to Fort
Clatsop to canoe the Lewis and Clark River. We saw a bald eagle, two deer,
and several ducks and geese and wished we'd been with the Corps of
Discovery.

Tongue Point, which Lewis and Clark knew as Point William, lies
on the south side of the Columbia River near present-day Astoria.

The Columbia River provided salmon for food along with sturgeon and
eulachon (also called candlefish). The adjacent forests provided timber to
build Fort Clatsop; firewood to burn for heating, cooking, and curing meat;
and elk for meat and hides. The clear-water streams that flow into the Columbia provided water for drinking and cooking and routes of travel into
the interior. The ocean tide and the river it churns twice daily provided
the medium of travel for hunting and fishing as well as for heading home
in the spring of 1806.

Once they got serious about traveling up the Columbia, they made 151
miles in nine days. They executed a seven-mile portage at The Dalles,
lined the empty canoes up the Narrows and carried their meager supplies
and trade good around the rapids. They lost one dugout in lining, leaving
them with only five canoes. On April 13, 1806, they traded two robes and
four elk hides for two Indian canoes to replace it. They had enough canoes
again, but they were struggling against a powerful river, flowing twenty
vertical feet higher than it had the previous fall.

By April 24, less than two weeks later, after trading for horses, they
abandoned the water route. Moving up the Columbia was too slow, too
dangerous. Above The Dalles they cut up their last two ponderosa pine canoes and one Indian canoe for firewood. The remaining canoes they had a
hard time selling. They split one for firewood to let the local Indians know

they would destroy the crafts rather than take a loss. They traded their last canoes for a few strings of beads.

A bridge now crosses the Columbia near its mouth; dozens of others cross its inland waters. Dams block its flow toward the ocean, and by doing so, block or delay the salmon and steelhead runs from returning to their spawning grounds, or their young smolt from reaching the ocean. Railroads and highways follow the course of the Columbia, giving modern travelers an inkling of what Lewis and Clark saw when they came this way two hundred years ago but little of what they experienced.

The three rivers the expedition followed from the base of the Bitterroots to the Pacific each had a different character: while the Clearwater flowed clear, the Snake had a greenish-blue color, and the Columbia, huge and powerful, was brownish with silt. They all hosted salmon in season, but the salmon runs had passed when the expedition arrived. The Corps of Discovery fed largely on dried salmon, roots, spoiled elk, and the flesh of dogs purchased from local Indians.

The land through which the three rivers ran varied as well. The Clearwater, a mountain stream, flowed through well-forested hills. The Snake, through a gorge cut into a barren basaltic plain. Their voyage on the Columbia began in similar terrain, but where the river cut through the Cascade Range, its character changes abruptly.

They found themselves on tidewater in a well-watered land where it rained almost constantly. Clark complained on November 15, 1805, of continual rain for ten days "without a longer intermition than 2 hours at a time from the 5th in the morning untill the 16th is *eleven* days rain."[22] Robert Cantwell records, in *The Hidden Northwest*, that "rain fell every day for thirty-one days" and that, "In the five months that Lewis and Clark were in the Northwest there were only twelve days without rain, and six of those were cloudy."[23]

A different climate, a different river. They never quite learned to adjust to the tide or to the rain. Initially, they found traveling against the tide worse than traveling up the Missouri. At Fort Clatsop they kept losing canoes to high tides, but when they headed up the Columbia in the spring of 1806, they learned to travel on the incoming tide that carried them upriver as it did Jack and me in April, 2002.

Only on the Columbia did they attempt to travel upstream during their return trip. When it became too frustrating, they left the river to travel overland on horses. They never did attempt to breach the flow of either the Snake or the Clearwater, even though high water had covered most of the rocks that had caused them so much grief the fall of 1805. The rivers west of the Divide served the expedition as a medium of transportation, but on their return trip, they abandoned the swift-flowing rivers that now impeded their homeward progress.

LEWIS AND CLARK EXPLORE SEPARATE RIVERS

To get a broader sense of the Rocky Mountain region on their return trip from the Pacific, Lewis and Clark explored separate rivers. Lewis by land explored rivers northwest of the Missouri's Great Falls, primarily the Marias and its founding branches. Clark, traveling first by land, then by river, explored the lower Gallatin and Yellowstone Rivers. The captains were still seeking that easy water route Jefferson had sent them west to find, and they had not fully satisfied themselves concerning the geography of the region's rivers.

The expedition divided into three main units, but at one time the various parties further split into five separate groups. Lewis, with only three men, explored the Marias while six members of his party remained at the Great Falls to help Ordway and his men portage canoes around the Great Falls and recover the caches. From the Three Forks, Ordway had split off Clark's party and led nine men down the Missouri in canoes. Clark and the remainder of the party traveled by horse to the Yellowstone, built canoes, and followed that river downstream to the Missouri. He sent Sergeant Pryor and three men overland to the Mandan villages with the horse herd.

Lewis's Exploration of the Marias

When Lewis and Clark parted company at Traveler's Rest in the spring of 1806, after crossing the Bitterroot Mountains eastward, Lewis led nine men to explore separately several rivers northwest of the Great Falls of the Missouri River. The Marias had both puzzled and intrigued the captains as they traveled up the Missouri. They had spent nearly a week at their confluence trying to determine which fork was the true Missouri, and which was merely a major tributary.

To review, as the expedition traveled west, at the mouth of the Marias, they had correctly chosen the left fork, had soon found the Great Falls, and had then discovered the Three Forks. During their trip westward across the mountains, they learned from Indians of a shorter route from the Great Falls to rivers flowing toward the Pacific, a route that might be the long-sought Northwest Passage. With Indian guides, Lewis's party split from the main party to explore this shortcut on horseback, then to follow the Marias to its source.

On the return trip Lewis followed the rivers as usual: first down the Bitterroot (Clark's River to the expedition), then across what Lewis called "the East branch of Clark's River" a few miles west of modern Missoula (it is now the Clark Fork, which flows into Lake Pend Oreille, the Pend Oreille River, in northern Idaho, and ultimately into the Columbia). They built three log rafts to effect the crossing, then traveled up the Big Blackfoot and its tributaries to what is now known as Lewis and Clark Pass.

On the way, Lewis and his men camped on Rattlesnake Creek (northeast of present-day Missoula) and crossed Gold Creek, Belmont Creek, and a Clearwater River (not the one in present-day Idaho). Then they crossed Hard Scrabble Creek and went up and across Alice Creek as they traveled slightly north of east toward the pass.

Once on the eastern side of the Continental Divide, they found themselves in the headwaters of the river they had named the previous fall for Secretary of War Henry Dearborn. They crossed a low ridge to Elk Creek, a tributary of Medicine (now Sun) River, and followed it to the Missouri. They had become familiar with the Medicine (Sun) River, which enters the Missouri in present-day Great Falls, a few miles above the head of the Great Falls, during their portage, hunting, and canoe building the previous summer.

From Traveler's Rest, Lewis had reached the White Bear Islands at the Great Falls of the Missouri in only nine days, a total distance of 184 miles. (From the Indians, he learned of an even shorter route that would reduce the distance by thirty-eight miles.) By contrast, on their way west the previous fall, the water route up the Missouri, Jefferson, and Beaverhead, then overland to Traveler's Rest had taken them fifty-eight days by a circuitous route of several hundred miles.

Once at the Great Falls but on the wrong side of the river, Lewis had the men kill several buffalo and build skin boats to cross the Missouri and open the upper caches left the previous year. Short of horses because some had strayed or been stolen, Lewis took only three men with him to explore the Marias headwaters: Drouillard as usual and the Field brothers. The others he left to help Sergeant Ordway with the portage and the recovery of their cached supplies, gear, and specimens.

Departing July 16, they crossed the Missouri and Medicine Rivers, swimming the horses and ferrying the baggage across in one of the skin boats. They headed downstream to camp near the forty-seven-foot falls (Rainbow), which Lewis sketched. The next morning (July 17) they traveled north toward the stretch of the Marias above which they had explored the previous year (Horse and Dugout Coulee). Lewis intended to travel far enough upstream to determine how far north and west it headed. They crossed the Teton River, which Lewis described in some detail.

Moving west, the men hunting and Lewis botanizing, they followed the Marias, crossing present-day Pondera Coulee and Willow Creek. Tiber Dam and Reservoir (Lake Elwell) mark the area today. Following Cut Bank Creek, the north branch of the Marias River, the four men reached a point about fifteen miles northeast of present-day Browning, Montana, within sight of the mountains of today's Glacier National Park. They spent several days waiting for the skies to clear so that Lewis could take astronomical readings. The skies never cleared. Lewis named their encampment Camp Disappointment before heading back toward the Missouri.

On July 26, 1806, Lewis saw about thirty horses with several Indians nearby; they seemed to be watching Drouillard, who was hunting along the river. Fearing that the Indians, seeing a lone white man, might attack him, Lewis made his presence known. They were a hunting party of eight Prairie Gros Ventres, according to Bob Saindon, though most scholars now believe they were Piegan Blackfeet.[24] They met and shook hands; Lewis gave the Indians a few small gifts. With Drouillard's help, they spoke and agreed to camp together. All went well through the evening as they smoked together and talked. Lewis told them the expedition intended to open trade with tribes who were enemies of the Piegan Blackfeet. This information may or may not have been a factor in events that occurred the next morning.

At daybreak the Indians made their move to steal the party's guns and horses. The Field brothers pursued the Indians and overtook them. Lewis tells the story: "R. Field as he seized his gun stabed the indian to the heart with his knife—the fellow ran about 15 steps and fell dead."[25]

Lewis also gave chase, threatening the Indians, raising his voice and rifle in all seriousness. One Indian stopped "at the distance of 30 steps from me and I shot him through the belly, he fell to his knees and on his wright elbow from which position he partly raised himself up and fired at me, and turning himself about crawled in behind a rock which was a few feet from him. He overshot me, being bearheaded I felt the wind of his bullet very distinctly."[26]

At one point Lewis had actually prevented the Field brothers and Drouillard from firing at the fleeing Indians, then he himself fired. The party had all recovered their rifles, but the Indians were getting away with some horses. It seems that Lewis shot the Indian for little more than stealing horses. To add insult to injury he left one of the expedition's medals on the bloody breast of the dead Indian, letting the Piegan Blackfeet know who had killed him, like Odysseus in *The Odyssey* telling the Cyclopes who had blinded him.

One Indian was dead, another seriously wounded. Although several of the expedition horses were missing, the men had saved their own weapons and had prevented the Indians from collecting their weapons and most of their horses. Lewis's party had enough horses to make an escape, which they did in a hurry, fearing that the Indians might bring a large party back to counterattack and avenge their lost warriors.

They lit out for the mouth of the Marias where they hoped to find the canoe party. Amazingly enough, they did find the Ordway (or canoe) party just as they reached the river, after having ridden more than a hundred miles in thirty hours. They escaped, but they left a negative impression on a tribe that Jefferson had hoped to bring into the American fold.

Clark's Exploration of the Yellowstone

The Yellowstone River flows north from its source in southern Yellowstone National Park across the Continental Divide from the headwaters of the Snake, which flows south, then westward to the Columbia. The expedition never saw the Yellowstone country that has been preserved as the nation's and the world's first national park, but a member of the expedition, John Colter, is widely credited with having discovered that land of lakes, rivers, waterfalls, wildlife, and geothermal activity.

Today, boating is prohibited on all rivers in the park except a short stream between Shoshone and Lewis lakes in southern Yellowstone called Lewis River, the only segment of the Snake River drainage that retains the *Lewis* name given it by the expedition.

The Yellowstone flows for 678 miles, most of it through Montana, the longest free-flowing river in the United States outside of Alaska. Aboriginal inhabitants called it Elk River. The Fischers describe three segments below Yellowstone National Park's northern boundary: the 103-mile-long mountain section from the park boundary to Big Timber, a 160-mile transitional section to the mouth of the Bighorn River, and the three hundred plus-mile prairie section from the Bighorn River to the Missouri.[27]

The mountain segment, a blue-ribbon trout stream, features Yankee Jim Canyon and Paradise Valley, a frequently floated stretch popular with fishermen and recreational boaters. In the transitional segment, Clark and his party reached the river, traveled along it on horseback, and built two canoes. They floated the entire prairie segment to the Missouri River as did Sergeant Pryor and his men in two bullboats.

After Captain Clark sent Sergeant Ordway down the Missouri River toward the Great Falls on July 13, 1806, he led the remainder of the party from the Three Forks up the Gallatin River, over Bozeman Pass, to the Yellowstone. The party included York, Charbonneau, and Sacagawea, who knew the route, and little Pompey as well as Sergeant Pryor, William Bratton, George Gibson, Hugh Hall, François Labiche, George Shannon, John Shields, and Richard Windsor plus forty-nine horses and a colt.

If Sacagawea served the expedition as guide, it was on this crossing from the Three Forks over Bozeman Pass to the Yellowstone, a forty-eight-mile stretch. Their route, an old buffalo trail used by the mountain tribes to access good hunting grounds to the east, was fairly obvious. The trip took only one long day, during which they made twenty-seven miles, and the shoulders of two other days (an afternoon and a morning).

Reaching the Yellowstone near present-day Livingston, Montana, they headed downstream on the north side of the river, looking for trees large enough to use for building canoes. After four days they located trees that would serve their purpose and built two canoes. They were in a hurry to rendezvous with Lewis and the rest of the party and to get back to St. Louis by fall. Clark kept a careful record of their descent, a total of 115 miles overland but 191 miles by water from where they'd first reached the Yellowstone to their canoe camp. While they built canoes, Gibson suffered a serious leg wound in falling off his horse, Indians stole half their horses, and wolves or dogs ate most of the meat they were curing—flesh from seven deer, eight elk, two buffalo, and a pronghorn.

In four days, two new canoes were ready. Clark had them lashed to-

William Clark's name and the date of his passage, carved into the
soft rock of Pompey's Pillar, remain for modern travelers to witness.
He named it Pompey's Tower for the son of Charbonneau and
Sacagawea. As a baby, Pompey accompanied the party, which
passed this rock their first day on the Yellowstone.

gether to create a safer craft, and on July 24 set out down the Yellowstone
by water. Sergeant Pryor and two men brought the horses along, still following the north side of the river. Clark and the canoe party made almost
seventy miles that day despite stopping to ferry the horseman's baggage
across the river. At Pryor's request, Clark sent a third man along to drive
the buffalo out of their path as the horse party headed to the Mandan villages. They didn't get far, but that's another story.

In the double canoes, Clark and his party covered fifty-eight miles their
second day on the river, taking time to explore a rock formation they
named Pompey's Tower after Sacagawea's baby. Clark carved his name
into the soft rock of the tower. The third day, they made sixty-two miles;
the next, eighty and a half. Their best day (August 2) they made eighty-
six miles, but on several days they traveled between forty and fifty miles,
upriver winds holding them back. They reached the Missouri on August
3, having covered more than six hundred miles in eleven days, averaging
fifty-six miles a day—they were hauling for home.

Chapter 8

TRAVELING UPSTREAM AND DOWN

Negotiating a river by human-powered boat at flood stage or on late summer low water offers problems enough, but traveling up the river against powerful currents seems next to impossible. The members of the Lewis and Clark expedition did just that: they traveled *up* the Mississippi for nearly two hundred miles in the fall of 1803, then *up* the Missouri for more than three thousand miles during five seasons. After wintering on the lower Columbia near the Pacific Ocean, they traveled *up* the Columbia for several weeks in the spring of 1806 on water much faster and more powerful than they had seen the previous fall when they had traveled down the Clearwater, Snake, and Columbia to the coast.

Before the advent of steam-powered boats or diesel engines, how did Lewis and Clark travel upriver against the strong currents of the Mississippi, Missouri, and Columbia Rivers? How did they deal with the hazards and overcome the obstacles they encountered? How did they handle such adversities as thunderstorms with their gusty winds, heavy rains, and pounding hailstones; herds of swimming bison blocking the river; hoards of mosquitoes; crumbling banks and quixotic sandbars? How did they even survive, much less move the heavily loaded keelboat and pirogues—and later, the heavy cottonwood dugout canoes—upriver?

BREASTING THE CURRENT

Their first encounter with breasting a powerful current occurred when they turned the point at the mouth of the Ohio River and headed up the

Mississippi in a keelboat and a small fleet of pirogues. Seriously short-handed, they struggled, zigzagging back and forth across the big river, looking for the upstream currents (eddies) that would ease their toil. Traveling eight to ten hours a day, they made fewer than sixty miles in five days. It was hard work and slow going.

But their major efforts to travel upstream came on the Missouri River, the Big Muddy, the spring, summer, and fall of 1804, and again the spring and summer of 1805. In the spring of 1806, they exhausted themselves traveling up the Lower Columbia, which was raging high with local rainfall and Cascade snowmelt. So frustrated did they become at the slow, arduous pace and hard work of upstream travel on the Columbia that they left the river earlier than planned, reverting to horseback travel. By then the party had relatively little gear and few provisions to haul. They no longer needed the carrying capacity of their canoes.

They used four techniques for moving the heavy keelboat upstream against the Missouri's strong current: sailing, rowing, poling (also known as setting or pushing), and towing (hauling the craft by brute force with a tow rope, also known as cordelling). They employed the same techniques in the pirogues plus possibly a fifth, paddling, their major method of powering the canoes, to ascend various rivers on their way west and to ascend the Columbia on their return the spring of 1806.

Traveling upstream against a four- or five-mile-an-hour current is hard work, whatever method is used. In forty-five years of running rivers I have frequently floated on currents of similar speed, though I rarely traveled upriver, except when I poled more placid streams in a modern lightweight canoe. On the Snake River in Hells Canyon I once floated twenty miles in two and a half hours, going with the flow (including Wild Goose Rapid where members of the Lewis and Clark party bought steelhead in the spring of 1806). That's an eight-mile-an-hour current. It's hard to imagine breasting that kind of force on the Missouri in a heavy keelboat, which Lewis and Clark scholar Donald Jackson called, "a useful but ungainly craft, a faithful wallowing drudge."[1]

Sailing is the least labor-intensive technique, of course, but it is also the most quixotic, depending on the presence, consistency, direction, and strength of the wind. Both paddling and rowing involve pushing water against moving water, a frustrating business at best, especially when the water is flowing in the opposite direction. Poling consists of applying power with a hand-held pole to the river bottom in one direction to move the craft

Paired thole pins (far left)
on the white pirogue
replica (foreground) are
for rowing; the mast, for
sailing. Poles and extra
oars are slung alongside
the captains' cabin on the
keelboat in the
background.

in an opposing direction. But what if the bottom is too deep for the pole or
too muddy to offer a solid purchase? Towing a craft offered a whole new
range of obstacles and frustrations. Expedition members used the techniques available, often in unison, whatever worked in a given situation.

What was the best way to move a craft upstream against a strong current? That depended on the kind of craft, its contours, hull design, size,
and weight; the depth of the river, and the composition of its bottom; the
speed of the current, and the quality of the wind; the topography and nature of river bank terrain; the composition of that bank and the kind and
amount of stream-side vegetation; and even the mental state of the men.

SAILING. On May 14, 1804, at 4 P.M., the expedition left Camp Wood, on
the east bank of the Mississippi, where it had spent the winter preparing
for the journey up the Missouri. Clark wrote in his journal for that date,
"Set out from Camp River a Dubois at 4 oClock P.M. and proceded up the
Missouris under Sail. . . ."[2] They made six miles, traveling one and a half
miles across the Mississippi, then four and a half miles up the Missouri.

Private Whitehouse gave more detail: "hoisted Sail and Set out in high Spirits for the western Expedition. We entered the mouth of the Missourie haveing a fair wind Sailed abt. 6 miles and Camped on the North Side."[3] They no doubt rowed as well to propel the heavy keelboat across the Mississippi and against the strong current of the Big Muddy.

On May 15, Ordway wrote, "fair wind later part of the day. Sailed Some."[4] The next day they again "set sail," a common journal entry, but whether a factual or figurative description we don't know. On May 26, "The wind favorable to day we made 18 miles."[5] However, on several occasions a strong headwind caused a layover day with no progress. On July 21, under a southeast wind, they sailed. Since the river flowed southeast at this point and they were traveling upriver, that is, northwest, the expedition had an upstream following wind. They made nineteen miles as they passed the mouth of the Platte.

On Sept. 30, 1804, well up the Missouri in present-day South Dakota, Clark wrote, "proceeded on under a Double reafed Sale."[6] With a good strong wind, they folded or rolled the sail to reduce the wind's effect. Sailing requires a mast and a sail, which both the keelboat and pirogues had. The keelboat was equipped with a thirty-two-foot mast that supported a wooden cross-spar carrying a square sail and rigging for a foresail, a smaller sail before (fore) or ahead of the mainsail that could be used as a spritsail. The crew hoisted the sail whenever the wind was right, that is, when it blew upstream, a frequent but not consistent event based upon the diurnal and nocturnal wind patterns. Certainly they sailed; occasionally but not consistently the captains offered specifics in the journals concerning the means of power they used.

Early in the expedition, the keelboat mast broke on an overhanging tree (June 5, 1804). They had good wind that day but without a mast, were unable to sail. They replaced the mast as they did the cross-spar (sprit) and numerous oars, poles, and paddles as each broke or wore out through use or were lost. Although they may have been the best-equipped expedition in history of exploration, as one writer has suggested,[7] they were living off the land, which meant repairing what they had with what they'd brought with them or replacing it with what they found along the river.

The pirogues and canoes also had masts and small square sails. While these smaller crafts were more often rowed, towed, or paddled, they too were sailed when the wind was right. The men even raised the sail in a canoe to take advantage of the favorable wind as they hauled the heavy craft by makeshift wagon on the portage around the Great Falls.

When the wind wasn't right, the smaller crafts were in greater jeopardy of sudden gusts and high winds than the keelboat and were more subject to waves splashing into the boats, even more likely to capsize. Several times during the trip up the Missouri the pirogues and canoes took on water from wind-generated waves or from rapids, and a few times they swamped or threatened to capsize. Once, only the mast and rigging kept one of the pirogues from turning completely upside down.

Expedition members, battling the strong downstream current of the Missouri, employed the upstream wind and used it whenever they could, whenever it blew from any downstream direction. They might tack (follow a zigzag course in the general direction of the wind) when the wind blew from a quartering angle, but there were quixotic sandbars and floating debris to dodge and point bars to avoid, riverbed snags to miss, and rapids to negotiate, a tricky business at best when they tried to sail and downright dangerous at worst.

The crew of the keelboat and the pirogues hated crosswinds and headwinds. Crosswinds whipped up the river's surface, splashing waves into the smaller crafts, often wetting supplies, and making the boats harder to steer. Stopping to dry gear cost them time and distance and frustrated the captains, but it gave the men a break from hard labor.

Occasionally, strong headwinds forced them to halt for the day, or to resort to rowing or poling, or at worst, bringing out the cordelle (rope or towline) to tow the craft from shore or through shallows, the most difficult task of all for the hard-working men. A strong gusty wind might wrest control of the craft from the tillerman, could capsize a small craft, or even send a craft off course and into an obstacle or some other dangerous situation.

On April 13, 1805, with nonswimmer Charbonneau at the tiller and a strong upriver wind, the crew of the white pirogue hoisted both sails, the standard small square sail and a spritsail. They were making good progress until a sudden squall hit and tilted the pirogue dangerously. Charbonneau, literally scared stiff, put the pirogue broadside to the wind and the waves, a dangerous situation. Drouillard saved the day by taking the tiller from the terrified Charbonneau as the other men in the boat brought in the sail.

On May 14, 1805, a year to the day after the expedition left Wood River, with Charbonneau again at the tiller, a sudden gust threatened the stability of the white pirogue. Charbonneau froze at the rudder, and "in stead of puting her before the wind, lufted her [turned the bow] up into it."[8] The wind blew the sail out of an attendant's hands, and instantly the wind laid the craft down, turning it on its side.

Only the rigging kept it from turning "topsaturva." It filled to within an inch of the gunwale. Cruzatte, one of the best rivermen, was at the other end of the craft, too far away to help. To break him out of his frozen position, Cruzatte threatened to shoot Charbonneau, who finally grabbed the rudder and stabilized the craft, which righted. The men bailed. Sacagawea's quick action saved important papers and gear.

As difficult as upstream travel became, it was much easier with a steady wind from an advantageous direction. At different times the wind was a help and a hindrance, but it certainly enabled them to sail much of the way up the Missouri and to make more miles, whenever it blew from an appropriate direction, than any other means of power.

ROWING against any strong river current is hard work. Even rowing downstream with the current is difficult against a strong upstream wind. A rower knows the wind is more powerful than the river's current when it takes more muscle and energy, due to wind resistance, to reset the oars for the next stroke than to pull the stroke through the water. Nicholas Biddle, who first edited the journals, wrote in a meeting with Clark that the keelboat was powered by "rowing 22 oars."[9]

Rowing involves oars operated from a fixed fulcrum point, an oarlock. In the days of Lewis and Clark, tholes, either single or in pairs, were used as oarlocks. A thole is a vertical thumblike appendage to which an oar is attached; it serves as a fulcrum point for rowing. Some early crafts used two thole pins with the oar set between them (see photo on page 111), but the Lewis and Clark keelboat used single thole pins set on wooden blocks attached to the gunnels. Clark's side-view sketch of the keelboat (January 21, 1804) clearly shows them; an adjacent listing of keelboat gear includes a sketch of a block with thole pin and the explanation, "T is pins to row by"[10] (photo on page 51).

⎯⎯⎯⎯⎯〰⎯⎯⎯⎯⎯

A thole (from the Middle English root tholian, *meaning to endure or bear) is a wooden or metal pin set vertically in the gunnel (the upper edge of a craft's side) to serve as a fulcrum. The keelboat and the*

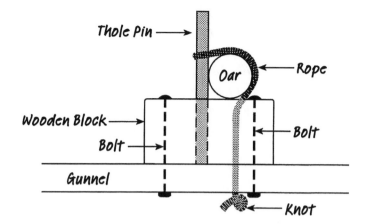

Sketch of thole pin and oar, by Heidi H. Hackler.

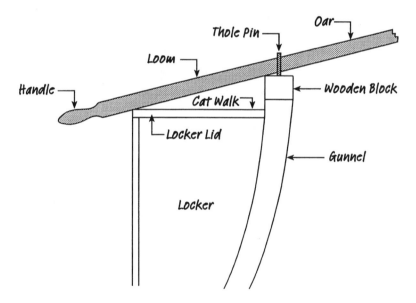

Sketch of oar and locker, by Heidi H. Hackler.

pirogues had thole pins for rowing. The keelboat had eleven sets of them. The pirogues must have had six and seven thole pins, perhaps paired sets of thole pins, respectively. Oars were probably tied to the thole pins with rope or rawhide. Without some kind of tie or attachment, the oars could not have been effectively or efficiently applied; they had to be married to the craft to be practical.

A fulcrum is a fixed point around which a lever moves. In the case of an oar (the lever), the oarlock or thole pin and its fixed seating provide the fulcrum. If you pull on the handle of an oar, the blade fulcrums in the opposite direction, pushing the water in that direction as the craft moves in a counter direction: the craft to which the oar is fixed moves in the direction of the handle or loom.

If the wind failed to blow, the men had to row, facing downstream and looking backward over their shoulders to see where they were going. Why? Because pulling on an oar is much more powerful than pushing on it, and in order to pull an oar to move the craft upstream, rowers had to face downstream, with the boat's bow pointing upstream.

One sergeant on the bow of the keelboat was assigned to keep a sharp lookout, not only to point the direction of the craft but to watch for obstacles—snags, sawyers, sleepers, sweepers—or debris floating in the river—logs, whole trees, animal carcasses—that might damage the keelboat or send it off course. In dangerous water, he held one of the poles ready to ward off any such obstacle. The larger (red) pirogue had seven oars and a crew of eight or nine men. The patroon (boss) held the rudder at the stern of the craft and served as lookout. When he discerned a problem, he called to the bow oarsman, who was in a better position to react, to leave his oar and deal with the problem. On the keelboat Cruzatte and Labiche alternated in that role.

The lookout for the smaller white pirogue, Corporal Warfington, commanded the craft and crew on the way up the Missouri to Fort Mandan. The white pirogue had a crew of six men including Warfington, who could not row, steer, and serve as lookout all at the same time. Each day the captains assigned an extra man from the keelboat to the white pirogue's crew. Just as Deschamps, the patron of the red pirogue, Warfington had to serve as lookout from the stern while he manned the rudder; when he saw a problem, he ordered the bow rower to deal with it.

It's hard to fathom rowing a large keelboat or a heavily loaded pirogue upstream against a four-mile-an-hour current. It requires a coordinated effort by a team of powerful men to row that fast in a rowboat on still water. Is there any wonder that the expedition rarely made more than a dozen miles a day when they had to row? Battling the Missouri's current, they sometimes made eighteen or twenty miles in a single day on an upriver wind, but they averaged fewer than ten miles a day fighting that powerful current, which Clark once calculated at 2.36 miles an hour. Some segments of the upper Missouri flowed much faster, but by then they no longer had the heavy keelboat.

They rowed often during the summer of 1804. Private Whitehouse, a rower and the journalist who offered the most detailed account of their mode of travel, reported their rowing mileage: July 1, twelve plus miles; July 5, ten miles; July 7, fifteen miles (that day, the sound of their oars startled a wolf sleeping on the riverbank); July 9, twelve miles; July 19, twelve miles; and July 20, seventeen miles. August 4 they rowed seventeen miles; August 5, sixteen.

On July 19, 1805, Lewis wrote, "altho' the current is strong it is not so much so but what it may be overcome with the oars for there is hear no possibility of using either the cord or Setting pole."[11] Sometimes the river was too deep or the bottom too muddy to pole, and often the bank offered no path for towing.

By contrast, on the downstream run, homeward bound the summer of 1806, they occasionally covered eighty or more miles a day. Their record was ninety-seven. On one stretch of the Beaverhead, they made as many miles in one day going downstream as they'd made in a week struggling upstream.

When the wind failed to blow or blew from the wrong direction, or when the force of the current was too powerful for the rowing crew, the men had to try something else to move their crafts toward their goal.

POLING is a technique that makes use of a long pole, one end of which is pushed against the river bottom. "Climbing the pole" may seem a ridiculous description, but it is the best way to describe the technique: a stationary poler places one end of the pole to the river bottom, then shoves against the bottom as he climbs hand-over-hand to the other end of the pole, exerting power against the river bottom.

A poler's feet never leave the deck. The climbing action simply exerts power to the river bottom, an action that moves the craft in an appropriate direction. The power of pushing off the bottom of the river is transferred to the craft through the soles of the poler's feet. It is a technique applied by native people all over the world. As old as the pyramids, poling has been used in Asia, Africa, Europe, and both Americas. It is used today by indigenous people in many third-world countries in their daily lives; it is used as well for river recreation in much of the modern world. It was a common practice in the early nineteenth century.

On the Lewis and Clark expedition, when the goal was to move the keelboat upstream, a crew of men in line began at the bow of the boat, which pointed upstream. Each man placed one end of a long pole on the river bottom, the other in his armpit (they did not climb the pole as a solo or tandem poler would), then walking slowly along the catwalk toward the stern, each pushed backwards against the river bottom as he moved forward (downstream), thereby forcing the keelboat upstream.[12]

The catwalk created by the locker lids fastened securely in the down position was lost if the lids were raised as a barricade against Indian attack as they were in the expedition's encounter with the Teton Sioux. After reaching the stern each man returned to the bow to repeat the process, hour after hour, all day long if the wind failed to blow or if it came from the wrong direction or grew too strong or too gusty. Poling was hard, grueling work that the men hated, but it was more energy efficient than rowing and better than towing, the technique at the top of the list of unpleasant jobs.

The pirogues could be poled as well, the men standing rather than walking, pushing backward against the river bottom, climbing the poles. If the riverbed were too muddy to offer the pole enough resistance, the technique was less effective. Occasionally a pole stuck in the muddy bottom or became entrapped between rocks or in woody debris on the river bottom, leaving the poler the choice of letting go of the pole or clinging to it in the middle of the river as the craft drifted out from under him. (There is no evidence in the journals that any such events occurred, but it seems likely, given my own experience at poling, for it has happened to me. The men often had to make or find new poles because they lost or broke them.)

The men of the Lewis and Clark expedition poled the keelboat at times, perhaps more frequently than the journals suggest. They stopped often to find wood to make new oars and poles to replace those broken, worn out, or left behind. They liked ash for oars but for poles no preference is given in the journals. They used abandoned tipi poles, usually lodgepole pine, at least once and found they worked well.

The secret to successful poling is splitting the current with the bow of the craft. When the bow parts the current exactly, the boat's drag is minimized as the current applies equal pressure to both sides of the craft. An old Nooksack Indian on his tribe's namesake river in northwestern Washington State, where I practiced poling myself, told me of tandem poling with his father. From the nearest store they tandem-poled a canoe to their cabin on the Nooksack's South Fork, a distance of six miles, in half an hour. That's traveling twelve miles an hour upstream against a strong current. Judging from my own experience, I have no reason to doubt his story.

I have never poled a keelboat, but I find poling a canoe much easier and more efficient than paddling one. On the Cowlitz River, a tributary of the Columbia, I kept pace with a marathon (downriver) paddler in a modern canoe, poling my own canoe as he plied a bend-shaft paddle. I was in my sixties at the time.

A technique generally considered the best way to move a craft upstream against a strong current, poling has proven itself in every quarter of the country from Maine to Mexico, from the Pacific Northwest to the Florida Everglades. Pushing off the stationary river bottom is more energy efficient than rowing or paddling against water moving rapidly downstream. It is a technique that the Corps of Discovery used regularly, often in combination with other techniques.

On July 23, 1805, Lewis wrote, "we made great uce of our seting poles and cords the uce of both which the river and banks favored."[13] The riverbed was firm; the river was shallow; and the bank was sound and bare of brush and trees. A few days later Lewis himself tried poling: "I occasionly encourage them by assisting in the labour of navigating the canoes, and have learned to *push a tolerable good pole* in their fraize."[14] The party made nineteen and a half miles by river that day.

TOWING. Towing involves pulling watercraft along a watercourse with a rope or cordelle from shore or from shallow water by horse-, mule-, oxen-, or manpower. The practice was essentially institutionalized a decade and a half after the Lewis and Clark expedition when the Erie Canal was constructed between 1817 and 1825. Its tow path alongside the big ditch facilitated teams of mules used to pull the barges along the route between Buffalo on Lake Erie and Albany on the Hudson River.

The initial crew of the keelboat used the technique to move the keelboat down the Ohio River late in the summer of 1803. Lack of rain had allowed the Ohio to shrink to its lowest level in four years. As mentioned earlier, Lewis was forced to hire teams of oxen or horses to tow the bulky but empty keelboat over shoals and through riffles—and that was going with the flow of the river though there wasn't much current. The men themselves, standing in the tepid water, lifted, pulled, and pushed the

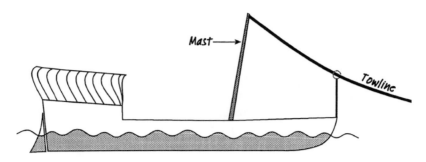

Sketch of towing arrangement for keelboat, by Heidi H. Hackler.

keelboat as best they could, often manhandling it downriver, but the job sometimes proved more than they could manage.

Later, on the trip up the Missouri, when the wind failed or the current grew too swift for rowing or poling, the men of the expedition had to resort to the towline, a dangerous and exhausting business. On July 7, 1804, Clark wrote, "passed Some verry Swift water on the L. S. [larboard side] which Compelled us to Draw up by the Cord."[15] In other words, they were forced by conditions to tow.

Sometimes they were forced to tow when there was no clear towing route and the water was too deep for the men to tow from the river. Then they had to cut trees and brush to create a tow path. Whitehouse, who did the towing and who provided the best details of their mode of travel in his journal, reported on June 26, 1804, that to tow they had to cut timber to create a tow path. On August 29, 1804, he reported that the party made a towing line from elk skins.

On May 17, 1805, Lewis wrote, "we employed toe [tow] line the greater part of the day; the banks were firm and shore boald [bald?] which favoured the uce of the cord. I find this method of asscending the river, when the shore is such as will permit it, the safest and most expeditious mode of traveling, except with sails in a steady and favourable breze."[16] Even given the conditions of firm footing, the men in the traces doing the hard work may have disagreed with their captain's assessment.

As Zadok Cramer warned in *The Navigator*, riverbanks frequently caved in from the current's undercutting action, sending the men on the towline down a bluff and into the river. Trees and underbrush often hindered the men's shoreline route. Badger dens, gopher holes, and beaver-cut stumps no doubt hampered them. Were they bothered by poison ivy? I find no mention of it in the journals, but I encountered it in abundance during a canoe trip on the middle Missouri between Nebraska and South Dakota in October, 2001; it may have been there when the expedition passed by. Such hazards as rattlesnakes, white-faced hornets, cacti, and sharp rocks made the men cautious, and the ever-present mosquitoes made them less effective in their towing (holding the tow rope, they couldn't swat the pesky beasts).

They stumbled on rocks and roots. Their tow ropes, especially those made of elk skins, broke, throwing the men about like losers in a tug-of-war contest and allowing the crafts to float down the river out of control, a loss of hours of hard towing, rowing, or poling. They often had to walk in the cold muddy water, bruising or cutting their feet on sharp stones, spraining ankles and wrenching knees as they slipped on moss-covered water-slick rocks.

Imagine their situation: they became hypothermic; their hands cracked from the silty water and dry air; they slipped and slid, scrambling up crumbling river banks; and they developed boils from long hours in the cold water, and dysentery from the muddy river water they drank. Mosquitoes were maddening, the sun hot and energy sapping. Men who suffered sunstroke during the summer, then suffered frostbitten feet in the winter at Fort Mandan. They wore out their clothes, went barebacked and barefooted. They endured the elements, but each day they advanced a few miles, perhaps a dozen or more when the wind was right.

On May 24, only ten days after leaving Wood River, the keelboat got into trouble in the Devil's Race Grounds. At this rapid the river flowed against some projecting rocks, which narrowed the river, thereby increasing the velocity of the current. As the crew towed from shore, the bank, undercut by the current, began to collapse. In trying to maneuver the keelboat, the men ran one end of the heavy craft onto a sandbar. The "barge" cartwheeled, broke the tow rope, and nearly capsized; and it would have, had the men on board not jumped into the shallow river and by sheer manpower kept her upright until the current demolished the sandbar by simply washing it away. They soon tied a rope to the stern, but it took men swimming to shore with a tow rope to recapture the runaway craft.

Massive river meanders created another frustration on the Beaverhead River in Shoshone Country where they made slow progress, primarily by towing. Sometimes the men could see across two or three loops of the river and realize they would have to pull the crafts two or three miles up the strong, shallow stream to make fifty feet across the meander. As reported, when I canoed this same stretch of the Beaverhead, I paddled twenty-six miles to cover the twelve road miles between the Beaverhead Rock and the city park at the edge of Twin Bridges, Montana. I too became frustrated and considered portaging, but I didn't, even though my canoe was much lighter than the cottonwood dugouts.

Think of the practical problem of getting men across the river when a cliff or bluff, a thick forest, or series of snags ended their tow route on one bank. They had to cross the river for a new purchase on the opposite shore. Here's where the lighter, more maneuverable pirogues earned their keep. While a towline tied to a tree held the keelboat in place, with perhaps a few men bracing it to keep it positioned to split the current, the other men were ferried by pirogue to the opposite bank with another towline. They would take up the slack while someone untied the fixed rope holding the keelboat; they would then tow her from the far side, often against an angling current until they gained a better purchase to split the current from the other bank. No journal entries describe this technique—it was standard procedure—but it must have happened time and again on the meandering rivers.

Despite Lewis's comments to the contrary, towing proved the most difficult method for the men to move the various crafts upstream, but it was often the only way to go. The men grew to hate it more than any other technique, but in certain circumstances, it had to be used.

PADDLING. Historian David Lavender wrote in *The Way to the Western Sea* that the men paddled as much as they rowed. Certainly they did not paddle the keelboat; it was too big and heavy, and the men were too far above the water for efficient paddling. Just as certainly they did paddle the canoes. Perhaps they paddled the pirogues some of the time, even though the larger crafts were designed and equipped to be rowed.

Despite the fact that the Lewis and Clark journal writers rarely differentiated between oars and paddles, they are different tools: oars are used for rowing and paddles are used for paddling. An oar makes use of a fixed fulcrum; a paddle makes use of the paddler's lower hand as a dynamic fulcrum. An oar stroke is more powerful and efficient than a paddle stroke because it has a fixed fulcrum, the oarlock or thole pin, which is married to the craft.

A paddle stroke is much more versatile because it can be applied in almost any direction, but an oar's fulcrum attachment limits an oar stroke to a single plane. Hand-held paddles lose some efficiency to the dynamic fulcrum provided by the paddler's lower hand, which moves. Thus they do not deliver their full power potential to the water, but they can be applied in any of several directions.

Native Americans do not speak of paddling a canoe; they refer to canoe pulling. Their concept follows this pattern: plant the paddle in the water and pull the canoe toward the paddle. In the same manner, plant the paddle in the water and pull or push or pry the craft in any direction. Most Native American paddlers use short narrow paddles at a pace well above a stroke a minute.[17]

The Lummi Indians of northwestern Washington are the only American tribe who participate in the War Canoe racing season in Puget Sound and southwestern British Columbia. From Mother's Day through mid-August they compete every weekend in a series of canoe races from solo and tandem canoes through four- and eight-person canoes to war canoes in which one person, often a small lightweight woman, provides the paddling pace by voice cadence. The war canoes are roughly fifty feet long, their outer surface so polished that "a fly can't stand up on one," as one Lummi paddler assured me.

When members of the Lewis and Clark expedition reached the mouth of the Columbia, they found the local natives using fine canoes highly superior to their own heavy dugouts. Lightweight and maneuverable with a carrying capacity greater than that of the expeditions' dugouts, the native canoes were powered by paddlers, often a dozen or more men. The women used smaller canoes for hunting, fishing, and food gathering.

Paddling was the basic technique used in the smaller crafts, the true canoes, and perhaps occasionally in the pirogues. The skin boats were paddled as well though the rafts were probably poled. No doubt the members of the Corps of Discovery learned a great deal from the Indians living on the Columbia, for they were superb canoeists.

When the expedition was pinned down by wind and wave at the mouth of the Columbia River, the local Indians visit them nearly every day, bringing food and trade items. Clark wondered at their paddling skills, writing (November 11, 1805), "Certain it is they are the best canoe navigators I ever Saw."[18]

Whatever technique the members of the Lewis and Clark expedition used to advance their crafts against the current, they practiced persistence, moving a few miles a day, or many, to achieve their goals. Heading downstream with the current, they had to learn new techniques and practice different patterns.

GOING WITH THE FLOW

The Lewis and Clark expedition is better known for its struggle upstream against the powerful currents of the Missouri River and its meandering headwater tributaries above the Three Forks than it is for traveling downstream with the flow. However, the expedition covered 5,498 miles traveling down various rivers, far more mileage that they accrued fighting the flow (3,548). They traveled much faster going with the current, but they encountered a whole range of new problems to address. It took them awhile to make the adjustments.

Following the flow involves different techniques from traveling against the current. Crafts move faster, a fact that reduces reaction time available to avoid obstacles. Faster current also increases the impact of crafts against obstacles, should they hit any, causing more damage and greater potential for disaster. Even landing a craft on shore requires different methods.

Traveling down the Ohio River in the fall of 1803 in the keelboat, the expedition had few impact problems because the river was low and slow. It did offer shallow water and shoals that were beyond the crew's capacity to manage without help, but that only slowed their progress; it did not create life-threatening situations. The river was low, the crafts undermanned and not yet fully rigged, and the crew was new to river travel. What lay in store for them west of the Divide when they would once again travel downstream they could only anticipate.

When they first encountered the rocky rapids of the Clearwater, Snake, and Columbia in the fall of 1805, the expedition had two years of experience on the river and was at full strength. Yet several factors created serious problems almost immediately. They had new untried boats and were traveling rivers new to them in a strange landscape, different from anything they had experienced. Accustomed to traveling upriver, against the current, they were now floating downstream on rapid waters beset with serious rapids in much steeper terrain.

Traveling downstream may seem easier than breasting a powerful river, and it is: the current does most of the work. It's a matter of going with the flow, unless the flow goes over a waterfall or through a serious rapid or on the wrong side of an island or into a pile of driftwood. Then you have to maneuver the craft quickly or stop it, an easier matter going upstream than down. River current slows a craft traveling against it, but a craft moving with the flow accelerates.

Negotiating rivers they have never seen before, boaters face hidden falls and unknown rapids, quixotic currents, hidden obstacles, and shore-line protrusions, all of which offer potential problems. Local natives told Lewis and Clark what they could about the river—which rapids to scout, how to run particular chutes, where to portage—but expedition members, using heavier crafts lacking wave-deflecting hull design, had to make their own decisions and learn from their own experiences and mistakes.

The faster the flow, the harder it is to stop the craft and the faster its crew has to maneuver to avoid obstacles. Which side of an island offers the better route? It may be difficult to determine if the island obscures the confluence of channels below or hides a rocky run-out from view. If a decision is not made early enough, a craft may be swept into a logjam on the point of the island that divides the river or may ground to a stop on a gravel bar that divides the current. (Read R. M. Patterson's *Dangerous River* and chapter 7 of his *Far Pastures* for examples.)

The expedition's most difficult downriver runs occurred on rivers west of the Divide during the fall of 1805. It was autumn and waters were low; rocks littered the channels, chutes narrowed, dark bedrock appeared to obstruct what would have been clear passages at higher water levels. Even worse, rocks called sleepers, hidden just beneath the surface, created imperceptible surface disturbances that caught boatmen off guard or "sleeping" and damaged boats or held them in the current.

I ran the Salmon River in early September when the flow was less than 2,000 cubic feet per second (cfs), roughly the level at which Clark had seen on the Salmon when he explored it at about the same time (the last week of August); he described it as "almost one continued rapid" and decided against attempting the river. Today, midsummer commercial trips on the Salmon run on water levels between 6,000 and 16,000 cfs. On our trip at 2,000 cfs, most passengers walked around major

rapids. It was dangerously rocky—as were the Clearwater and Snake
for the Lewis and Clark expedition in the fall of 1805.

⸻

Traveling downstream in their heavy new dugout canoes on the Clear-water, Snake, and Columbia, the expedition crews paddled for the most part. They rarely rowed or poled because the river provided plenty of power, and sailing would have been unnecessary, dangerous, and counter-productive against powerful winds blowing up the Columbia River Gorge. Occasionally they let the canoes down with ropes, but they had little need to tow the crafts except when they became stuck on a sleeper or between rocks, and then only to free them from the current's pressure.

On the return trip, once they had crossed the Continental Divide they made good time traveling down the Missouri and its tributaries: the Beaverhead and Jefferson, and for Clark's crew, the Yellowstone. In fact, they often made in a single day as many miles as it had taken them a week or more to travel upstream. Not only were they familiar with the river, but they were also heading home and going with the flow.

Each downstream trip exhibited unique problems, as evidenced by four different segments of downriver travel: the eleven-hundred-mile trip down the Ohio River the fall of 1803; a 640-mile trip down the Clearwater, Snake, and Columbia the fall of 1805; Clark's 636-mile trip down the Yellowstone the summer of 1806; and a 3,096-mile return trip from the canoe cache on the Beaverhead to St. Louis during the summer of 1806.

Down the Ohio (autumn, 1803)

The voyage from Pittsburgh, where the keelboat was built, to the Missis-sippi, where the expedition first turned upstream, served as a shakedown cruise for the keelboat, as a training run for the men, and as a reality check for the captains. Three pirogues augmented the keelboat's carrying ca-pacity and gave the expedition the flexibility to explore. The pilot hired to master the keelboat took it through the Falls of the Ohio; at least one pirogue was manned by a hired hand.

Lewis started keeping his journal on the downriver run of the Ohio in the fall of 1803. So did Clark once he joined the expedition at the Falls, where he lived at the time. Because of serious low water, the keelboat car-ried little equipment and few supplies for the upper few hundred miles.

It served its purpose on the lower Ohio, and it delivered many of the expedition's crewmembers to Wood River, where the expedition wintered and from which they launched their attack on the Missouri the following spring.

Once they reached deep water, they drifted with the current, making eighteen or nineteen miles a day. They had too few men to do much rowing, and we are not even sure they had thole pins in place on the keelboat "to row by." They did have oars and poles and probably used them to augment the current's push by poling, but at that time the boat had no catwalks. If they poled at all, they likely poled while standing. They did use the sail when the wind was right, but they made relatively poor time for a downriver run (they experienced considerable upriver wind).

Still, there were no major problems once they passed the Falls of the Ohio at Louisville. Their pilot left the party below the Falls, but Clark was now on board and usually in charge of the keelboat. He knew more about boats and river travel than Lewis did.

As Robert E. Hartley points out, Clark had spent considerable time on the Ohio and Mississippi Rivers before the expedition.[19] In the militia, in 1789, he had first crossed the Ohio to pursue Indians. When he was in the army during the fall of 1795, he had traveled down the Ohio and Mississippi to New Madrid on military business. Later, as a civilian on legal business for his older brother, George Rogers Clark, in 1797, he had spent several weeks in the Illinois country (Vincennes, Kaskaskia, Cahokia) where the expedition wintered. He had also crossed the Mississippi four times and visited St. Louis.

The expedition spent two weeks at Clarksville, loading provisions and adding men to the crew. They headed downstream on October 26, and reached Fort Massac, Illinois, on November 11 to add more crew, including George Drouillard, who helped recruit men for the permanent party. On November 14, they reached the Mississippi and camped on the point between the two rivers. From here it was upstream all the way to the Continental Divide.

Down the Clearwater, Snake, and Columbia (autumn, 1805)

Using five canoes made from ponderosa pine trunks, the Corps of Discovery made excellent mileage paddling down the Clearwater, Snake, and Columbia Rivers in October and November of 1805. Nights grew cold;

water levels were low. Rocks that had been covered by water at higher river levels appeared above the surface, narrowing channels; others hid just beneath the surface, dangerous "sleepers" waiting to grab a canoe if its paddlers failed to observe the river's subtle signs.

On October 7, they left Canoe Camp across from the Clearwater's North Fork (now blocked by the massive Dworshak Dam, which eliminated the largest natural steelhead run in North America). Almost immediately they ran into serious problems. Clark's canoe struck a rock in the third rapid and sprung a leak; they made twenty miles. Overnight they repaired the damaged canoe, and Clark moved to a different craft. The second day Sergeant Gass's canoe hit a rock, split, and sank, injuring John Thompson in the spill. Despite the accident, they made twenty-one miles.

They spent the third day drying goods and baggage wet on the previous day and repaired the canoe. On October 10, they reached the Snake, having covered sixty miles in three travel days. They made half that many miles their first day on the Snake, and passed nine rapids without mishap. Perhaps they were learning the subtleties of downstream travel.

On October 12, they passed several rapids requiring "maney turns necessary to Stear Clare of the rocks, which appear to be in every direction,"[20] wrote Clark. They made twenty-three miles. Clark admits they took chances by not scouting more rapids: "We Should make more portages if the Season was not So far advanced and time precious with us."[21] The same day he commented on Sacagawea's role in the party: "The wife of Sharbono our interpetr we find reconsiles all the Indians, as to our friendly intentions a woman with a party of men is a token of peace."[22]

On October 14, they had one of their worst accidents (see chapter 7, River Incidents). Drouillard's canoe struck a rock, broached, and sank; several men clung to midriver rocks and held the canoe against the current. The men and canoe were saved, but much of the load was lost and everything was wet, including loose powder and a large quantity of "prepared roots" recently purchased from the Indians to feed the crew.

Shortly before reaching the Columbia two days later, Sergeant Pryor's canoe hit a rock and stuck there, the men climbing out onto the rock in midriver. With the assistance of three other canoes, Pryor and his crew were rescued, but again most of their load was wet. Clark walked around this rapid. They'd come 140 miles in six days on the Snake and Clearwater.

The Columbia is a mighty big river. In the next six days they covered

Beacon Rock, described by Lewis and Clark (November 2, 1805),
lies immediately below Bonneville Dam. It still marks the upper
extent of tidal influence on the Columbia River. They remarked on
passing it again on April 9, 1806, on their return voyage.

154 miles, portaging a bad rapid to Strawberry Island (part of the modern
Bonneville Dam). They portaged Celilo Falls and ran the short and long
narrows at The Dalles (all inundated by modern dams). They soon
reached tidewater and a new obstacle to thwart their travel plans: the
Pacific tide. They had to gauge their daily launch to coincide with the tidal
flow, for paddling against the tide was similar to paddling against the upstream current, but riding the outgoing tide sped their progress.

The lower Columbia was a nightmare. The river widened and slowed.
It became too brackish to drink; they now depended on rainwater and
side streams for drinking water. The upstream winds near the Columbia
mouth stalled their progress; conflicting tides confused them. Waves and
ocean swells pounded their primitive dugouts, filled them with water,
wetting them and their supplies, which they could not dry due to the constant rain.

Pinned down by the waves and weather for days, they explored the
north shore and found it less than desirable as a winter camp. They moved
back up the river to a narrower section where their crossing to the south

shore was protected from ocean swells, wind, and wave action by a series of islands (now the Lewis and Clark National Wildlife Refuge, where Jack Remington and I canoed in April of 2002).

Finally, on a tributary that flows into a shallow bay on the south shore near the mouth of the Columbia, they found a reasonable place to build a winter camp. They named the structure Fort Clatsop for a local Indian tribe. They wouldn't travel down another river until they crossed the Divide on their way back to the United States.

Down the Beaverhead, Jefferson, and Missouri (summer, 1806)

The return trip by boat down the Beaverhead and Jefferson Rivers in the summer of 1806 involved only Clark and his party, about two-thirds of the expedition members. As indicated earlier, Lewis had left the main party at Traveler's Rest on July 3, at the eastern foot of the Lolo Trail, to explore the Marias headwaters. Clark led the rest of the party to the canoe cache on the Beaverhead, which they reached on July 8.

Two days later, after recovering and air-drying the canoes and opening the caches, Clark's party launched the canoes carrying their baggage and provisions, heading for the Three Forks. Six men under Sergeant Pryor traveled overland with the horse herd to meet them. Clark wrote that the canoes traveled as fast as the horses, but the next day the canoes outdistanced the horse herd.

The canoe party camped opposite the mouth of the Big Hole, near present-day Twin Bridges, Montana, where the Jefferson River begins at the confluence of the Beaverhead and the Big Hole. The small canoe they'd left there the previous year the men cut up for firewood. They had little to carry and were in a hurry.

To illustrate the hazards of downstream travel on fast mountain rivers, on July 12, Clark's canoe "got drove to Shore by the wind under some tops of trees [sweepers] and was near being filled with water," as Ordway wrote. Clark "fired 2 guns as a Signal for help"; the other canoes stopped to render assistance and "Soon got him Safe off."[23] Howard was injured slightly in the accident. They proceeded on to the Three Forks, which they reached July 13.

After they had lunch together, Clark sent Ordway and nine men in six canoes down the Missouri. Then, with the rest of the party and forty-nine horses, he headed overland to explore the Yellowstone River. As mentioned, Ordway led the nine men to the Great Falls to meet the crew left by Lewis to help dig up the caches and portage the canoes around the falls, then reclaim the pirogues below. Only Ordway's journal provides the details of that part of the journey. As Clark and his party traveled up the Gallatin and over a low divide to the Yellowstone, Sacagawea, who knew the route, may have led the way. They followed that river for four days, then built canoes and floated it to the Missouri.

Back at the Great Falls, after reaching the White Bear Islands on July 11, Lewis took three of his men north to explore the source of the Marias. He left the others to help with the portage when Ordway arrived with the canoes. Lewis had intended to travel with a larger party, but when several horses strayed or were stolen by Indians, he took only the Field brothers and Drouillard.

From the Three Forks, Sergeant Ordway continued down the Missouri through the Gates of the Mountains, fighting severe headwinds in the narrow canyon. High winds nearly filled one canoe with breaking waves; mosquitoes and flies gave the men misery. They reached the White Bear Islands July 19, six days after leaving the Three Forks, and found Sergeant Gass with five men of Lewis's party to help portage, which, assisted by horses, they accomplished with relative ease in less than a week (it had taken nearly a month to portage the falls the previous summer).

Once around the portage and back on the Missouri below the falls, the party recovered the white pirogue, found it in good shape, made a few minor repairs, and loaded it and the five canoes with baggage and specimens. By midday July 27, they headed downriver.

It's a good thing they did, for the next morning Lewis and his three men, running from a fight with the Piegan Blackfeet on the upper Marias, arrived, having ridden 120 miles in thirty hours. Timing is everything in sport or in lifesaving. Lewis wrote, "on arriving at the bank of the river had the unspeakable satisfaction to see our canoes coming down."[24]

Later that day they recovered the red pirogue but found it so badly decayed that they abandoned it and proceeded down the Missouri, camping on the right (south) bank as protection against the Indians they were sure were following. They were now in the white cliffs and stone walls area, today protected under the National Wild and Scenic Rivers Act and as a national monument. A severe thunderstorm followed by an all-day rain filled the Missouri with so much mud Lewis found the water difficult to drink. [Thunderstorms I experienced the summer of 2002 as I canoed this stretch of the Missouri also muddied the river and made a morass of one of our campsites.]

They found the Missouri mellow, the wildlife abundant, hunting productive. They killed fifteen elk and fourteen deer in one day, "and took their skins," for they no longer had any goods to trade (so much for Lewis's claim that they only killed enough to eat). They needed hides to bargain with the Mandan for food. On August 4, Ordway and Willard, caught on the river after dark, had an encounter with "a parsel of sawyers" but survived (see chapter 7, Incidents). On August 11, the one-eyed, nearsighted Cruzatte accidentally shot Lewis in the buttocks, but Lewis too survived. At 1 P.M. the next day the entire party rejoined and headed for the Mandan villages and St. Louis.

Down the Yellowstone (summer, 1806)

Shortly after Clark and his party crossed the low mountain gap now known as Bozeman Pass, they reached the Yellowstone River. After following it for four days, they found cottonwood trees large enough to build canoes. The party hollowed them out with ax and adz, since they were too green to burn; it took them only four days.

Sergeant Pryor still headed the horse party, reduced to three men after they lost roughly half the herd to Indian horse thieves. Clark headed downstream with his party in the two canoes lashed together, sending Pryor with the horse herd down the left (northwest) bank of the river. They met downstream, the canoe party crossing over the baggage of the horse party to keep it dry, while the horses swam the river. Pryor requested an additional man to handle the horses, and Hall, a nonswimmer, volunteered. The horse party headed eastward overland toward the Mandan villages, and the canoe party again moved downriver.

On the river they made good time, covering seventy miles the first day, fifty-eight the second, and sixty-two the third. They were moving down a swift-water river with few serious obstacles. They settled down to a forty-three-mile-a-day average, then went sixty-six miles on July 31. They traveled like a horse heading for the barn after a hard day's work. On August 2, they made eighty-six miles. The next day they reached the Missouri, found the mosquitoes intolerable, and moved downriver. They stopped to hunt, to dry meat, and to cure hides, which they planned to trade to the Mandan for food.

Arrival of Sgt. Pryor, by John F. Clymer. Reproduced with
permission of Mrs. John. F. Clymer and the Clymer Museum of Art,
Ellensburg, Washington.

On August 8, they were joined by Sergeant Pryor and his trio (Shannon,
Hall, and Windsor). All the horses had been stolen on their second night
out. They had hiked back to the river, killed some buffalo, cut some willow sticks, and made two bullboats after the manner of the Mandan and
Arikara. They entered the Yellowstone near Pompey's Pillar, floated the
Yellowstone to the Missouri, and followed Clark's party to the point where
they caught up with Clark.

The Missouri River below the Mandan villages offered the returning
expedition no real problems. Upriver winds slowed them, occasionally
stopped them for a few hours, and there were the usual thunderstorms,
but the hard parts of the trip were over. There were no serious rapids, and
the problems they encountered going up the Missouri were so many
pieces of cake on the downriver run.

Chapter 7

RIVER INCIDENTS

Rivers served the members of the expedition as friend and foe: they threatened them and saved them, kept them alert and alive, enabled them to travel relatively easily but periodically created problems. Some problems were merely humorous; others, life-threatening. A few nearly stopped their journey.

Two incidents occurred on May 14, 1805, a year to the day after the expedition left Wood River, that typified their problems on the river. The first involved a grizzly bear attack in which the river saved the men; in the second, the white pirogue suffered a mishap in which the river nearly ended the expedition. The accident "had like to have cost us deerly," wrote Clark, for they almost lost important papers and critical instruments as well as much of their medical supplies. A sudden wind actually caused the accident, but the river current compounded it, making it dangerous, even life threatening.

Grizzly Attack

In the first incident, "the men in the canoes Saw a large brown bear on the hills on S. S. [starboard side] 6 men went out to kill it,"[1] as Ordway, an eyewitness, wrote. Three men fired while the others waited; they had learned that grizzlies were hard to kill. As they had anticipated, the wounded bear attacked. The others fired but failed to stop the wounded beast. It chased two of the men back to their canoe.

Following them into the water, the bear almost caught them, but as the

Hasty Retreat, by John F. Clymer. Reproduced with permission of
Mrs. John. F. Clymer and the Clymer Museum of Art,
Ellensburg, Washington.

canoe found the current, it carried them downriver to safety. Ordway
wrote, "he [the bear] took the River and was near catching the Man he
chased in, but he went up againt the Stream and the bear being wounded
could not git to him."[2] After killing the bear with a shot to the head, they
examined it and found that eight rifle balls had struck the animal. It took
a shot to the head at close range to kill the huge beast. This happened
about 4 in the afternoon.

Capsize

About 6 P.M. another incident, alluded to earlier, occurred: "a Squawl of
wind Struck our Sale broad Side and turned the perogue nearly over, and
in this Situation the Perogue remained untill the Sale was Cut down in
which time She nearly filed with water,"[3] wrote Clark. He added, "the articles which floated out was nearly all caught by the Squar [squaw] who
was in the rear. This accident had like to have cost us deerly; for in this perogue were embarked our papers, Instruments, books, medicine, a great
proportion of our merchandize, and in short almost every article indispen-
sibly necessary to further the views, or insure the success of the enterprize
in which, we are now launched to the distance of 2,200 miles."[4]

Lewis didn't bother to mention Sacagawea's quick thinking, her rescuing papers and other items floating about, but he provided more detail: "a sudon squawl of wind struck her [white pirogue] obliquely, and turned her . . . before the wind, lufted her up into it, the wind was so violent that it drew the brace of the squarsail out of the hand of the man who was attending it, and instantly upset the pirogue and would have turned her completely topsaturva, had it not been for the resistance mad by the oarning against the water."[5]

Charbonneau, a nonswimmer and "perhaps the most timid waterman in the world," according to Lewis, had been at the helm, a unique situation, for he was not a trusted sailor. However, during the day's confusion he had been entrusted with the rudder. Cruzatte, the more experienced riverman, could not reach the rudder from his position in the bow to correct Charbonneau's inappropriate steering; he threatened to shoot the interpreter to get him to grab the rudder, steer the swamped craft, and correct the mishap.

As mentioned before, a similar incident a month earlier should have forewarned the captains not to trust Charbonneau at the helm. On April 13, the white pirogue was under sail before a strong following wind when "a suddon squall of wind struck us and turned the pirogue so much on the side as to alarm Sharbono who was steering at the time, in this state of alarm he threw the pirogue with her side to the wind, when the spritsail gibing was as near oversetting as it was possible to have missed."[6]

Drouillard saved the day, taking the rudder from the petrified Charbonneau, and the pirogue "was agin plased in a state of security." Three nonswimmers plus Sacagawea and her baby were all on board as high waves threatened the craft two hundred yards from shore. It could have been a disaster, but as often happened, they came through without serious results. Clark, exploring on shore, missed the event.

Flash Flood

On June 29, 1805, a flash flood almost swept several key members of the party into the river above an eighty-seven-foot drop at the Great Falls. Clark led Charbonneau, Sacagawea with their baby, and York to visit the spectacular Great Falls, which had so enraptured Lewis a few days earlier. Caught in a sudden thunderstorm that generated torrential rains and huge hailstones, they sought shelter in "a deep rivene where there were some shelving rocks under which he [Clark] took shelter near the river with

Sharbono and the Indian woman,"[7] wrote Lewis. Clark laid his gun, compass, and other gear under a rock ledge to protect them from the rain.

Clark took up the story: "Soon after a torrent of rain and hail fell more violent than ever I Saw before, the rain fell like one voley of water falling from the heavens and gave us time only to get out of the way of a torrent of water which was Poreing down the hill in the rivin with emence force tareing every thing before it takeing with it large rocks & mud, I took my gun & Shot pouch in my left hand, and with the right Scrambled up the hill pushing the Interpreters wife (who had her Child in her arms) before me."[8]

Losing virtually everything they had with them, they climbed out of the ravine before the fifteen-foot wall of water, mud, stones, and brush swept past them. They lost the large compass, gun, tomahawk, shot pouches and powder horn, the baby's clothes, several pairs of moccasins, even Clark's umbrella. When they reached the plain above, they saw York, who had been hunting for buffalo, looking for them, "greatly agitated, for our wellfar."

On the Salmon River, the expedition's East Fork of Lewis's River, I experienced a similar flash flood but fortunately was not caught in it. Camped at Lantz Bar, our party had just settled in for the night when a hard rain began. As darkness fell and the rain increased, we heard a low rumble that sounded like a freight train, but no railroad tracks desecrate the wild and scenic Salmon River, the same river Clark had explored in the hope of following it to the Pacific. It grew louder, trembling the earth. The last light of dying day reflected on Little Squaw Creek as it entered the eddy below our boats.

Suddenly the light disappeared as the reflection vanished in a mass of muddy water. Rocks, logs, whole trees came charging into the eddy. Soon we saw dark objects floating in the eddy, but everything seemed to flow downstream; the water level of the eddy did not rise. After the flash flood subsided our expedition discovered mud on tree trunks eight feet above the ground five feet from the creek. The bridge across the creek had washed away. Next morning the mouth of Little Squaw Creek was mired in mud three feet deep, and the Salmon River flowed muddy for the remainder of our week long trip.

Cold, wet, and muddy, the flash-flood survivors staggered back to camp on Willow Creek, which had risen six vertical feet during the storm, and found that the men hauling baggage across the eighteen-mile portage had been caught in the open by the same storm. Huge hailstones had beaten and bloodied several of the nearly naked men; two of the men had been knocked down, one of them three times. Several hailstones weighed three ounces each; one measured seven inches in circumference. [During the summer of 2002, similar-sized hailstones fell a few miles from our campsite on the upper Missouri when a tornado touched down nearby.]

Rocky Rapids

When the expedition launched onto the Clearwater River, they were in a hurry. It was late in the season and the water was low with many rocks showing and the current swift. The expedition grew careless in their rush to reach the Pacific before winter arrived; they didn't know what to expect from the weather or the river. They did not scout rapids and suffered the consequences. Clark admits as much: "We Should make more portages if the Season was not So far advanced and time precious with us."[9]

Their canoes were untested, and the men hadn't been on the river for several weeks. They had grown accustomed to traveling against the current, but now they were going with the flow, facing a different set of circumstances. Weakened by near starvation, illness, and a radical change of diet—from fresh red meat to dried salmon, pounded roots, and berries—they had problems almost immediately. The day they left their Canoe Camp (October 7, 1805), the canoes struck rocks, hung up on others and "obliged us to get out in the Water (that was cold) and hawl them off," wrote Whitehouse, the only private whose journal remains. The officers' canoe "leaked so bad, that they were forced to unload it, & put their baggage into another Canoe, for fear of getting their Mathematical Instruments & baggage wet."[10]

On their second day, Clark relates that one of the canoes nearly turned over, sprung a leak, filled with water, and sunk in a rapid, endangering the men. Whitehouse offers greater detail: "one of the canoes Struck a rock and wheled round then Struck again and cracked the canoe and was near Spliting hir [her] in too. throwed the Stearsman over board, who with difficulty got to the canoe again, but She soon filled with water, and hang on the rocks in a doleful Situation."[11]

The expedition faced rocky rapids, which gave them serious
trouble, on the Clearwater, Snake, and Columbia Rivers.

The men unloaded a canoe and, with the help of Indians in another canoe, saved the men and most of the baggage though all were wet. They
saved the canoe, repaired it overnight and dried the bedding and trade
goods. Gass wrote simply, "I had my canoe stove, and she sank. Fortunately the water was not more than waistdeep so our lives and baggage
were saved, though the latter was wet."[12]

The Corps of Discovery reached the Snake River, where the rapids were
worse. On October 14, 1805, Clark wrote, "three Stern Canoes Stuk fast for
Some time on the head of the rapid and one Struk a rock in the worst part,"
but all got safely off. However, later the same day "our Stern Canoe in passing thro a Short rapid opposit the head of an Island, run on a Smoth rock and
turned broad Side, the men got out on the [rock]. . . . The Canoe filed and
Sunk, a number of articles floated out, Such as the mens bedding clothes &
Skins, the Lodge [the tipi in which Lewis and Clark and the Charbonneau
family camped] &c. &c. the greater part of which were cought by 2 of the
Canoes, wilst a 3rd was unloading & Steming the Swift Current to the relief
of the men on the rock who could with much dificuelty hold the Canoe."[13]

Of this accident Gass wrote, "a canoe hit a rock, and part of her sunk, and a number of things floated out. With the assistance of the other canoes all the men got safe to shore; but the baggage was wet, and some articles were lost."[14] Again Whitehouse offered more detail: "ran fast on a Solid rock and Swung across the rock."[15] The men stepped out of the canoe onto the rock and attempted to shove her off. They could not budge her, at first, then the lightened canoe moved off the rock so suddenly it left four men stranded in "water half leg deep over the Smooth rock" in the middle of the rapid. The men were rescued by other canoes, the baggage was wet, and some items were lost.

On the Rio Chama in New Mexico, when my canoe struck a rock in Upper Gauging Station Rapid, it swung sideways and caught another rock, broached, and wrapped around the second rock. I perched alternately on the rock and in the swamped canoe; Carl, my paddling partner, found footing in the waist-deep water. My canoe shifted, then split and hung fast. Rod Nash, following in a small cataraft, threw us a safety line. With three of us tugging, we could not extract the canoe from the rock. We cut the tie-ropes to free our gear, but the current swept it out of the canoe and into the river before we could grab all of it. Using the throwline, Rod pendulumed us, one at a time, to safety.

While the expedition salvaged most of their gear and saved the dugout, we lost my canoe, my tent, rain gear, and assorted camping equipment; Carl lost his lantern, camp stove, and ice chest with our remaining food. Between us we lost a thousand dollars worth of equipment and ruined my wife's camera, which I'd borrowed for the trip.

The Columbia itself exhibited serious rapids and falls, which the party had to portage. On October 22, 1805, they reached Celilo Falls, a drop of thirty-seven feet, a traditional fishing place for the local tribes. The men portaged the baggage that day, then "Took the Canoes over the Portage on the Lard. Side with much dificuelty . . . one Canoe got loose & cought by the Indians which we were obliged to pay,"[16] wrote Clark.

It became a difficult portage: "I with the greater part of the men Crossed in the Canoes to opposit Side above the falls and hauled them across the portage of 457 yards with is on the Lard. Side and certainly the best side to pass the canoes."[17] Clark offers more detail concerning the canoe's getting away: "we were obliged to let the Canoes down by Strong ropes of Elk Skin which we had for the purpose, one Canoe in passing this place got loose by the Cords breaking, and was cought by the Indians below."[18]

In the Dark

On August 4, 1806, on the homeward stretch of the upper Missouri, Ordway and Willard in a small canoe stopped late in the day to hunt. They killed a deer and a grizzly bear. By the time they had taken the skins and what meat they needed, the sun had set. They proceeded on in the dark (Ordway says "by moon light," but see below). According to Ordway, they found themselves "in a thick place of Sawyers as the current drawed us in and we had no chance to git out of them So we ran about half way through and the Stern run under a limb of a tree and caught willard who was in the Stern and drew him out as the current was verry rapid. he held by the limb   I being in the bow of the canoe took my oar [paddle] and halled the bow first one way and the other So as to clear the Sawyers and run through Safe and paddled the canoe to Shore."[19]

Anyone who has tried to control a canoe from the bow can no doubt sympathize with Ordway, who ran back upstream trying to find Willard, left dangling from the sawyer, his arms wrapped around the limb, his feet kicking water. They made voice contact but could not see each other. Willard had caught some driftwood, made a small raft, and negotiated the current through the sawyers. Ordway launched the canoe "and took him in as he Swam through Safe." (The moon on that date was five days past full; it didn't rise until after midnight by which time they were off the river in camp.) For all its nonswimmers and time spent in the water and on the water, expedition members made a remarkable record of surviving the river's travails.

Crossing the Clark Fork

Lewis experienced a close encounter with the river now known as the Clark Fork (Lewis called it Clark's river) on his shortcut to the head of the Great Falls during the return trip. His party swam their horses across,

The Lewis Crossing, by John F. Clymer. Reproduced with permission
of Mrs. John. F. Clymer and the Clymer Museum of Art,
Ellensburg, Washington.

but to keep their baggage dry, they built three log rafts to ferry the river,
120 yards wide at the crossing. Lewis crossed with two nonswimmers: "the
raft by passing so frequently had fallen a considerable distance down the
river to a rapid and difficult part of it crouded with several small islands
and willow bars which were now overflown."[20] The July 3 date suggests
high-water time on the Clark Fork: it was in full flood.

Lewis and the two men "set out on the raft," which drifted a mile and
a half in the swift current before it reached the opposite bank. "On our
approach to the shore the raft sunk and I was drawn off the raft by a bush
and swam on shore the two men remained on the raft and fortunately ef-
fected a landing at some little distance below."[21] He wet his chronometer
(watch), but all three men came through safely.

Battered on the Beaverhead

After Clark led the party back to the canoe cache on the Beaverhead, he
traveled downstream in a canoe rather than follow the river on horseback.
Their first day back on the river, "the Canoes passed Six of my encamp-
ments assending"[22] and covered ninety-seven miles. By passing in one day

A log lying at river level beneath a spruce tree sweeper suggests the
problem Clark had on the Beaverhead.

the six camps of the previous fall, they made as many miles in a single day
as they'd made in a week battling the current.

Their third day on the river, "the Wind rose and blew hard off the
Snowey mountains to the N. W. and renderd it very difficuelt to keep the
canoes from running against the Shore," wrote Clark; "at 2 P. M. the Canoe in which I was in was driven by a Suden puff of wind under a log which
projected over the water from the bank [a sweeper], and the man in the
Stern Howard was Caught in between the Canoe and the log and a little
hurt."[23] This kind of accident often occurs to modern paddlers, the result
of the ways of wind and water.

Clark continued, "after disingaging our selves from this log the canoe
was driven imediately under a drift which projected over and a little abov
the Water, here the Canoe was very near turning over we with much exer-
tion after takeing out Some of the baggage hauled her out, and proceeded
on without receiving any damage."[24] Of the incident, Ordway wrote, "the
Canoe Capt. Clark was in got drove to Shore by the wind under Some tops
of trees and was near being filled with water. Capt. Clark fired 2 guns as a
Signal for help."[25] Other members of the party came to Clark's assistance
to extract his canoe from the sweepers.

Indian Troubles

One of the expedition's goals was to contact Indian tribes along the route and bring them into the fold of the American traders, to open commerce with the Indians. Jefferson naively hoped to bring peace to the western plains. Lewis and Clark ran into trouble with several tribes, especially the Teton Sioux.

Two aspects of the expedition's encounter with the Teton Sioux (September 25–28, 1804) bear telling: negotiation with tribal leaders and negotiation of the river. The first had more potential for disaster than any other meeting between the Americans and the native people. It could have ended the expedition. The captains had expected trouble with this band led by three principal chiefs—Black Buffalo, the Partisan, and Buffalo Medicine—who wrangled with each other in their quest for tribal power and sought to control commerce on the upper Missouri.

To a large extent they had been successful.

Aware of that tribe's strength and economic potential, Jefferson had informed Lewis that, "we wish most particularly to make a friendly impression [on the Teton Sioux] because of their immense power."[26] Virtually everyone Lewis and Clark had interviewed about the Teton Sioux told them to expect trouble from this tribe. The expedition found trouble and left a negative impression.

After an initial amicable meeting, the Sioux became surly and "troublesome," jostling Clark and offering "insulting jestures." The parley became a confrontation when three Brulé warriors grabbed the pirogue's bowline and another locked his arms around the pirogue's mast. Clark drew his sword; Lewis ordered the men to prepare for action. Some two hundred Sioux warriors stood ready with bows drawn as the expedition men primed their guns. At this point a pirogue full of armed American soldiers arrived, momentarily changing the balance of power. Sensing a double massacre, the chiefs relented. Black Buffalo tried to make amends and became friendly again but would not shake Clark's hand. The chiefs asked to see the keelboat, were ferried out to board it, and spent the night on the big boat.

The next day, to impress Lewis and Clark, the Indians invited the expedition to an all-day feast followed by a scalp dance that evening, celebrating their recent victory over the Omaha. One of their twenty-five

Omaha captives told Cruzatte, who knew the Omaha language, that the Sioux planned to kill the Americans, information that put the expedition on guard and once more increased tensions.

As the expedition members returned to the keelboat for the night, the Partisan and several of his warriors accompanied them in the white pirogue. None of the journal writers say who was steering, but whoever it was made a clumsy approach to the keelboat. The pirogue slammed against it and broke the anchor cable; both vessels began to swing dangerously in the current, careening down the river out of control.

Clark's call for the crew to man the oars awakened the Indians on shore. Thinking that the Omaha or the Americans were attacking, the Indians quickly armed and lined the riverbank, ready to defend their chiefs. Fortunately the chiefs intervened and no attack occurred.

Quick action by both parties temporarily averted violence, but tensions rose. In another morning of wrangling with the tribe, the battle of wills continued when several of the Partisan's warriors again grabbed a bowline. Lewis ordered the Indians off the keelboat; Clark grabbed the firing taper for the swivel gun. Violence again seemed imminent, but Black Buffalo defused the situation once more, and the expedition sailed on, leaving behind a confused and angry tribe that Jefferson had especially wanted the expedition to befriend.

James Ronda suggests that, "The last minutes of the Teton encounter were less a conflict between Indians and American explorers and more a tussle between rival band headmen."[27] In any event, the expedition failed to impress the Teton Sioux favorably and failed to accomplish the president's desire.

Other River Incidents

On May 15, 1804, the full expedition's second day on the Missouri, "the Boat run on logs three times to day"[28] and though "the barge was several minutes in eminent danger,"[29] got free. She was loaded too heavily in the stern. The water was rapid and the banks were falling in from their being undercut by the swift current.

On May 24, they ran the Devil's Race Grounds where, "The Swiftness of the Current wheeled the boat, Broke our *Toe* rope, and was nearly over Setting the boat, all hands Jumped out on the upper Side and bore on that

Side untill the Sand washed from under the boat and wheeled on the next bank   by the time She wheeled a 3rd Time got a rope fast to her Stern and by the means of Swimmers was Carred to Shore."[30]

On June 9, 1804, in "current exceedingly strong," the keelboat struck a hidden log and plowed into a mass of driftwood and snags with great force and ended up in the path of huge trees bearing down on them. The men leaped into the river, swam ashore with a rope, and "fixed themselves in Such Situations, that the boat was off in a fiew minits," as Clark wrote. He continued in praise of the crew: "Our party is not inferior to any that was ever on the waters of the Missoppie [they had only been on the river about three weeks, but Cruzatte and Labiche had already whipped them into a competent crew]."[31]

On June 29, 1804, "Passed a verry bad place of water, the Sturn of the Boat Struck a moveing Sand & turned within 6 Inches of a large Sawyer, if the Boat had Struck the Sawyer, her Bow must have been Knocked off & in Course She must hav Sunk in the Deep water below."[32] The keelboat missed the sawyer, and they proceeded on.

On July 14, 1804, a severe storm struck the keelboat nearly broadside. The boat's strong cable and anchor barely kept the boat from heeling over, and again the men jumped into the river to keep the boat from being thrown onto a sand island and "dashed to pieces." Clark wrote of a forty-minute "parel" [peril] in which a pirogue all but swamped; the keelboat itself was saved from swamping only by the men raising the locker lids and covering them with a tarp to keep out the waves.

On August 28, 1804, the red pirogue "like to have sunk" after she ran on a snag, which punctured her hull. An examination proved her "unfit for Service," and the captains decided to send her back down river. However, that didn't happen. On that date, Ordway wrote that the large [red] pirogue was blown ashore, got a hole knocked in her, and the keelboat came to her assistance. The following day he wrote that they had repaired the red pirogue, put some of its load in the white pirogue, and somehow it kept going. He also said that while the pirogue was being repaired, the men made a towing line out of green elk hides.

The white pirogue had its problems as well, so many that Lewis began to write about her "evil gennii." On May 5, 1805, Lewis wrote, "soon after seting out the rudder irons of the white pirogue were broken by her running fowl on a sawyer, she was however refitted in a few minutes with some tugs of rawhide and nales."[33]

On May 31, 1805, he calls the men's labor "incredibly painful and great" towing "in water even to their armpits." Then "The toe rope of the white pirogue, the only one indeed of hemp . . . gave way today at a bad point, the perogue swung and but slightly touched a rock, yet was very nearly upsetting; I fear her evil genni will play so many pranks with her that she will go to the bottomm some of those days."[34]

One other bear problem seems worth mentioning: at the return portage, a grizzly attacked Hugh McNeal, whose horse, frightened by the bear, threw him. McNeal hit the bear over the head with his rifle, breaking the stock and stunning the bear long enough to give McNeal time to climb a tree. The bear had him treed for several hours before giving up; McNeal returned to camp after dark, shaken but unhurt, all in a day's work.

Incidents like these peppered the expedition's daily life, kept the men alert, and challenged their ingenuity. Nearly every day some little event occurred that made the voyage interesting, if not to the men of the expedition, then certainly to modern readers. Their river incidents often mirror the experiences of present-day river runners who have encountered rapids and swamped canoes, capsized and wrapped boats, gone swimming unintentionally, fought bears, and found themselves at the bow of a canoe out of control.

Chapter 8

OFF THE RIVER

Although the expediton spent many months traveling by river, twice they left the rivers to cross the Continental Divide, and twice they left the river to portage around the Great Falls of the Missouri. Once they left the river to take a useful shortcut. They spent more than a year in winter camps, waiting to get back on the river. In addition, the winter snows in the Bitterroot Mountains delayed them for a month, forcing them into a temporary spring camp on the Clearwater.

PORTAGES AND CROSSINGS

The expedition left the rivers several times: to portage around the Great Falls of the Missouri (twice); to cross the snowy Bitterroots and Continental Divide (twice); and to speed its return by taking a shortcut across the Snake River Plain. Separately, Lewis and Clark explored two areas off the main course of the rivers they had been ordered to travel; these side expeditions are covered in chapter 5.

Even when the expedition traveled overland, rivers played crucial roles, both positive and negative. They offered bounty and barrier, ease and exasperation, comfort and vexation. The expedition lost as much time gathering stray horses on the overland routes as they did waiting out contrary winds on the river. When they traveled by land, rivers became barriers they had to cross. Massive loops and numerous meanders frustrated them on the rivers by adding miles to their journey just as rivers thwarted them when they moved across the land, cut by depressions and gorges and blocked by deep, swift streams.

Rivers had carved the routes of travel that the expedition followed across the landscape. Snow that blocked their overland route melted to provide water for those same rivers. On their overland treks, streams provided water for the expedition, its horses and dog. They supplied food: fish in the water, animals that came to streams to drink or to cross to greener pastures. They found crayfish, waterfowl in adjacent wetlands, fruits, roots, and berries growing in the floodplain.

Headwater streams of the Bitterroot Mountains, and the streams that crossed the high barren plateau of the portage route and the shortcut across the Snake River Plain, provided both route and barrier, but the streams helped the expedition survive. Even when rivers failed to provide the medium of travel, they assisted the expedition in finding its way and sustaining its members.

On the Way West

PORTAGING THE GREAT FALLS. On the westward portage around a 360-foot series of major waterfalls on the upper Missouri River, the expedition spent almost a month hauling boats and baggage, supplies and equipment overland by sheer manpower. The Great Falls became the first major barrier to their travel across the continent by water. They manhandled the heavy dugout canoes for a mile and a half up Portage (now Belt) Creek before hauling them overland on crude wheeled carts, becoming beasts of burden as they pushed and pulled the heavy crafts along the eighteen-mile route. In addition to making wheels for the cart by cutting boles from a large cottonwood that grew near the river, they used the white pirogue's mast for axels. When it broke, they replaced it with scarce but soft local timber.

Each stream cut created a vertical break in the plain: the men eased their burdens down to the creek, crossed it, then hauled them back up to the plain. Willow Run (now Box Elder Creek), a small willow-lined stream, became their relief point; it served as both respite and curse, a water break and a refuge for grizzly bears.

One of the most frightening events of the expedition occurred on a small creek that cut into the high bench of the portage route, the flash flood that almost swept Capt. Clark, Charbonneau, Sacagawea, and her baby into the river and over the falls (see chapter 7, River Incidents).

This replica of an expedition dugout canoe being hauled over the portage route at the Great Falls of the Missouri resides at the Lewis and Clark Interpretive Center at Great Falls, Montana.

Grizzly bears plagued the men as though the huge bruins sought vengeance for the expedition's intrusion. The expedition members named a cluster of islands at the upper extremity of the portage trail White Bear Islands because so many grizzlies congregated there and attacked the men in an almost daily routine. Joseph Field flushed three grizzlies out of one thicket; one chased him off a steep bank onto a stony river bar where he fell, cut his hand, bruised his knee, and bent his rifle, but he did escape. The expedition devoted one day to a bear hunt simply to rid the area of the menacing grizzlies.

Mosquitoes, as usual, were bothersome, and prickly pear cactus became a serious problem, crippling the men as cactus thorns stabbed their feet through the moccasins they wore. Rattlesnakes were abundant; so were buffalo, a steady source of meat but a problem as well. The rains that created the flash floods soaked the ground so completely that when the vast herds of buffalo trampled the terrain into a quagmire, it dried and hardened to an all but impassibly rough surface.

The biggest disappointment at the portage was the failure of the iron boat, which was intended to replace the carrying capacity of the cached pirogues. Above the Great Falls, the iron frame fabricated at the Harper's Ferry arsenal was fitted with an animal-skin covering. Called the leather boat by Lewis, the *Experiment* was designed to haul a four-ton load. Four or five men could carry it. Caulked with a mixture of beeswax, charcoal, and buffalo tallow, the unique craft initially "lay like a perfect cork on the water," but the cold water and a hard wind caused the caulking material to separate from the hides and "left the seams of the boat exposed to the water and she leaked in such manner that she would not answer."[1] Lewis was mortified.

The expedition stalled only momentarily: the captains ordered the men to build two more dugout canoes. The hunters had seen trees large enough to serve the purpose only a few miles above the Falls, more than twenty miles by river but only eight miles through the woods, bypassing the meanders. While Clark with a crew of ten men set to work, Ordway began shuttling baggage in four of their dugout canoes as Lewis supervised the dismantling of the iron boat and the caching of supplies and goods for which they lacked cargo space. Five days later and twenty-three river miles upstream, the party proceeded on. The Great Portage was behind them.

CROSSING THE BITTERROOTS. On the way west the expedition found the Shoshone Indians when they needed them most, and by good fortune it happened to be a band headed by Sacagawea's brother, Cameahwait. Lewis and Clark needed horses, and in Sacagawea they had an interpreter who knew the language of the people who had horses. While Clark explored Salmon River (East Fork, Lewis's River), hoping to travel all the way to the Pacific by water, Lewis traded for horses. His ace in the hole was a promise of future trade with the Shoshone, including their getting guns for hunting and for defense against the Blackfeet and Hidatsa, who had already acquired them from the British.

Advised by both the Shoshone and Clark's reconnoiter against taking the water route, the expedition followed the Salmon downstream on horseback to its North Fork, then the North Fork upstream toward what is now known as Lost Trail Pass, a triple divide including headwaters of the Bitterroot, Big Hole, and North Fork of the Salmon Rivers.

Rivers that had shown the expedition the route to travel became barriers, which had to be forded when they traveled overland by horseback.

Led by Shoshone guide Old Toby, they descended to the Bitterroot River and followed it downstream where they met a tribe of friendly Flathead or Salish Indians at Ross' Hole heading toward the buffalo country for their fall hunt. The expedition obtained more horses and traded a few of their lesser mounts for better ones. Always they followed the river routes except over the passes where few streams ran.

Just south of modern-day Missoula, Montana, they turned sharply left toward the Bitterroot Mountains, where the network of small creeks along the Lolo Trail became a maze that on the way west even confused Old Toby, their Shoshone Indian guide. The steep country and constant ups and downs of the route were wearying and wearing. Now the streams became barriers they had to ford.

In mid-September they had snow. Clark's packhorse fell and crushed his writing desk. Finding little game except a few deer and grouse and the ubiquitous beaver, they nearly starved. They ate some of their horses and named a stream Killed Colt Creek.

In the higher country, where few creeks ran because they were frozen, the party melted snow for drinking water, using it for the "portable" (dehydrated) soup Lewis had brought along. One day they made only seven miles; most days they made no more than twelve or thirteen. On September 17, Clark wrote, "passed three Dreans [drains] to right and Encamped on one to the left. Springs at all these drains."[2] Whitehouse characterized one of those springs as "a Sinque [sink] hole full of water."[3]

The next day Clark with six men tried to break through to the low-lands in the Clearwater drainage. With an early start, they made thirty-two miles, saw a distant valley, but killed nothing for food. "Encamped on a bold running Creek passing to the left which I call Hungery Creek as at that place we had nothing to eate,"[4] wrote Clark.

The following day (September 19) Clark and his men hit Eldorado Creek and descended it to warmer weather. Still in the mountains, Lewis commented on birds and berries and bemoaned the loss of the packhorse with his winter clothing. His men ate grouse, coyote, crawfish they found in the creek, and "horse beef." The same day Clark met the first Nez Perce, who gave him and his party roots, dried salmon, and berries, a com-bination that sickened the near-starving men.

Clark sent a packhorse, led by Reuben Field and loaded with roots and salmon, to the party's relief. On September 22, Lewis and the rest of his party reached the first Nez Perce village. A day's travel ahead of him, Clark "found the Chif [chief] in a Canoe Comeing to meet me   I got into his Ca-noe & Crossed over to his Camp on a Small Island at a rapid."[5] They were on the Clearwater River, and the westward crossing of the Great Divide was history. The small creeks had shown them the way and had saved them.

Heading Home

Anxious to get back to the United States, Lewis and Clark started east ear-lier than they had planned, driven inland by the steady rain and poor liv-ing conditions at the mouth of the Columbia. They headed up that pow-erful river, but before reaching the Snake, they left it to travel overland along the north side of the river. They found trying to move upstream on the Columbia at spring high-water levels too time consuming and back breaking, even for this tough crew: too many portages, too swift and dan-gerous the current, too windy.

SNAKE RIVER SHORTCUT. When they found horses in Indian camps along the river, they began trading for them. Initially they had little luck, but gradually they acquired twenty-three horses. On April 19, they used four-teen of them to help with a portage. That day they cut up the last two large canoes made on the Clearwater to use for firewood; the same day the salmon arrived and the expedition was treated to the first salmon ceremony.

When I mediated a dispute between the Lummi Tribe and Whatcom County near Bellingham, Washington, in the early 1980s, I witnessed this ceremony: the first salmon caught is symbolic of the following run; the native people offered thanks to it for returning to feed them, then baked it over an alder-wood fire, each tribal member receiving a piece of the sacred fish as they sang and danced to honor the First Salmon. The skeleton of the fish was then returned to the river in a ceremonial gesture to enable the salmon to return to its ocean pasture and grow new flesh to perpetuate its life and continue feeding the people. The Lummi also played the common Native American stick or bone game that the captains described in the journals.

The worst rapids in the Columbia were drowned by the high water. Lewis wrote on April 23, "the water at present covers most of the rocks in the bed of the river."[6] At this point the expedition had only two crafts left, both Indian canoes, manned by Gass and Reuben Field in one, Potts and Colter in the other. The next day they traded the canoes for strands of beads, and the party began traveling overland along the river's north side. They made twenty miles the first day, twenty-eight the second, then thirty-one, much better mileage than they'd been making on the river.

There was one problem: they were on the wrong side of the river. Opposite the Walla Walla River, they met their old friend Yelleppit, chief of the Walla Walla, who gave Clark "a very eligent white horse" and offered to ferry the expedition across the Columbia. They swam the horse herd across while Yelleppit's canoes took the party and its baggage to the east side where they camped on the north bank of the Walla Walla River near its mouth (April 29, 1806).

From here they traveled across the Snake River Plain, short-cutting the great loop of the Snake River through what has become southeastern Washington State. Delayed by gathering their scattered horses, the party made only fourteen miles their first day through "an open sandy plain," camping on the Touchet River, a Walla Walla tributary. The following day, May 1, they made twenty-six miles following the Touchet, the easy route.

Collecting horses all the next morning, the party did not start until after noon; they made nineteen miles, following a "well-timbered creek" on which they found deer, crane, and beaver. The creeks once again provided food and firewood, water and route. The day after, with an early start and a cold tailwind, they made twenty-eight miles "through a high plain," enduring rain, hail, and snow; they camped on another creek in a cottonwood grove, which offered shelter from the wind. Here they meet a Nez Perce chief, Looking Glass, whose grandson of the same name would become a major participant in the Nez Perce War and Exodus of 1877.

On May 4, they reached Alpowa Creek and followed it downstream to the Snake, where again they found themselves on the wrong side of a river without a means of crossing. As before, they swam the horses and "we . . . pass the river . . . with the assistance on three indian canoes"[7] and camped a few miles below the mouth of the Clearwater. They followed its north bank over the next few days, deep into Nez Perce country, and set up a month-long camp, which a century later Elliott Couse named Camp Chopunnish, a title that was not used by expedition members but one that has stuck better than Lewis's name applied to the Snake River.

CROSSING THE BITTERROOTS. They reached the Nez Perce country too early to cross the Bitterroot passes. The snow was too deep, the land still locked in winter, a frustrating delay. They would have to wait a month to proceed. And so they did. Finally on June 10, anxious to be on the way, they moved from their temporary camp on the Clearwater River to Weippe Prairie and beyond in an attempt to cross the Divide but were turned back by twenty- to thirty-foot snowdrifts. They retreated, hunted and butchered, and smoked and dried meat for the trek across the mountains. Two weeks later, on June 24, they tried again and succeeded, taking six days instead of the eleven required going west.

Again they followed the creeks: Collins, Eldorado, Dollar, Hungry, then over the snowy pass and down to Glade and Lolo creeks, then Lolo Hot Springs, and Traveler's Rest where they relaxed and recuperated. This time they had been better prepared. It was spring in the high country, and they had sixty-six horses, "each man being well mounted and a light load on a second horse."[8] They even had spare horses. They found more food than they had the previous fall. On June 13, the hunters killed eight deer. They gigged salmon that had just begun running in the creeks west of the divide, and the hunters harvested bear, grouse, sandhill crane, even duck eggs. Nearsighted Cruzatte found morel mushrooms.

Still, they had a tough time in the steep terrain. They found Hungry Creek "difficult and dangerous to pass [cross] . . . in consequence of its depth and rapidity."[9] John Colter and his horse were swept down this creek, tumbling over and over together in the swift current, but both somehow survived their trashing.

Lewis wrote (June 26) that they traversed "the steep sides of tremendious mountains entirely covered with snow except about the roots of the trees. . . . we ascended and decended severall lofty and steep hights but keeping on the dividing ridge between the Chopunnish [North Fork, Clearwater] and Kooskooske [Lochsa] rivers we passed no stream of water."[10] They sucked snow for water until they reached flowing creeks at lower elevations.

They lost time collecting their horses several mornings but saved time because now they had Nez Perce guides who knew the way. They found good grazing for their horses on south-facing slopes; hard-packed snow made for easier travel over downed jack-strawed timber. At one camp their guides entertained the expedition with fireworks by setting fire to tall fir trees, which exploded into flames towering high into the night sky.

I remember driftwood fires set by river runners in Glen Canyon before the dam: to eliminate drift logs in the river, which later high water might free, boatmen would set fire to gigantic masses of driftwood lodged on beaches. The fires would heat the whole canyon, light the canyon walls generating weird shadows on the cliffs, and burn all night, making excellent coals for breakfast cooking if you could get close enough to use them.

They had not yet crossed the Great Divide between the waters of the Pacific and Atlantic, but the Bitterroot Mountains were behind them. Soon they reached the homeward side of the Divide by different routes (Lewis over Lewis and Clark Pass, Clark over Gibbon Pass) heading back to the United States, but they still had miles to go, initially overland on horses but ultimately back to the river that had brought them west. The rivers always showed them the way.

Going Separate Ways

When the expedition reached Traveler's Rest on Lolo Creek at the eastern base of the Continental Divide, as mentioned earlier, Lewis and Clark split the party: Lewis headed northeast to the Great Falls by a more direct route that would save them weeks of travel. Clark led the rest of the party back to their canoe cache on the Beaverhead where they recovered the canoes and returned to the Three Forks. Here Clark left the canoe party in Sergeant Ordway's capable hands to take down the river and portage the Great Falls while he led the remainder of the expedition to the Yellowstone (see chapter 5).

PORTAGING THE GREAT FALLS. Only Sergeant Ordway's journal provides an account of the return portage: neither Lewis nor Clark was present, and Whitehouse had either stopped keeping his journal or it has been lost. The expedition's most consistent journal keeper, Ordway provided many of the expedition's most critical details and some of the more astute observations.

From the expedition's canoe cache on the Beaverhead, Ordway led the boat party to the Three Forks, although Clark was in command. The canoe party paused once to rescue Clark from a dangerous situation (see chapter 7). From the Three Forks, Clark led a third of the party overland to the Yellowstone (chapter 5) as Ordway led nine men in the canoes to the Great Falls to execute the portage: Collins, Colter, Cruzatte, Howard Lepage, Potts, Weiser, Whitehouse, and Willard. They fought headwinds, and killed a mountain lion and many rattlesnakes, but with good hunting, they ate well even before they returned to buffalo country.

When they arrived at the White Bear Islands on July 19, they found six members of Lewis's overland party—Sergeant Gass, another journalist, and five privates (Frazer, Goodrich, McNeal, Thompson, and Werner)—plus four horses waiting to help with the portage. The early-arriving party had already opened the upper caches. As soon as Ordway arrived, they began planning the portage. Grizzly attacks resumed almost immediately as described in chapter 7. They laid over a day to recuperate and get organized. Tormented by flies and mosquitoes that swelled Ordway's eyes and face, they assembled the wagons and prepared to get under way first thing the following day. Now that they had horses to help and knew the route and the routine, it should have been easy, but the next morning they found only two horses and spent most of the day looking for the others. They got two canoes started down the portage trail with much of the baggage.

It was easier going downhill; they controlled the descent of the loads to avoid an accident that might have caused a runaway. They badly needed all the canoes they had for the trip back to St. Louis. Axles broke, cart wheels shattered, Weiser cut his leg badly and couldn't work. It rained, muddying the route and raising the creeks. Eventually they got all the canoes and baggage to the river below the falls, then uncovered the lower caches and recovered the white pirogue. They loaded it and headed down river. While the upstream portage had taken nearly a month, on the return trip they accomplished the task in a week.

The Lewis and Clark expedition certainly was a river trip, but even when the party traveled off the river, streams and creeks slowed their progress but showed them the route, provided them with food and water, gave them direction and a sense of safety, even protected them from the elements. As capillaries in the human blood system supply cells with nutrients and flow into larger veins, so the smaller streams of the Corps' overland routes sustained expedition members and fed rivers that carried the Corps of Discovery across the continent.

WINTER CAMPS AND SPRING RETREAT

A basic pattern of military life has long been "Hurry up and wait." The Lewis and Clark expedition followed that pattern, hurrying down the Ohio River the fall of 1803 only to wait out the winter at Camp Wood. They spent the following spring, summer, and fall hurrying up the Missouri River (if averaging fewer than ten miles a day can be considered hurrying) only to wait nearly five months in the bitter cold of a northern plains winter at Fort Mandan on the upper Missouri.

Then they hurried up the Missouri, across the Continental Divide, and down the Clearwater, Snake, and Columbia to reach the Pacific in mid-November. They waited in the rain of a Pacific Northwest winter at Fort Clatsop until the spring of 1806 before heading homeward. Anxious to return to the United States after two years in the "wilderness," they were delayed once more by deep snows on the Bitterroot passes.

Existing conditions forced the expedition to play the waiting game, even for short periods when contrary winds halted their progress. But because some rivers along the route froze during winter months, the party had to wait for spring thaw to travel. As they traveled overland by horse, snows on the mountain passes delayed them.

They stopped for the winter three times during their journey across the continent, each time establishing their quarters on a river: first, on the east bank of the Mississippi near St. Louis the winter of 1803–1804; second, at Fort Mandan on the upper Missouri the winter of 1804–1805; and third, on a Columbia River tributary near the Pacific Ocean the winter of 1805–1806. Finally on their return eastward, they were delayed for a month on the Clearwater River in Nez Perce Country, waiting for spring. They spent a lot of time in what the army calls "garrison duty," waiting, staying busy doing the mundane and finding food.

WOOD RIVER. As mentioned earlier, the expedition spent the winter of 1803–1804 camped in southern Illinois opposite the mouth of the Missouri some twenty miles northeast of St. Louis. Here the captains organized the expedition that traveled across the continent. The men lived on Wood River from December 13, 1803, to May 14, 1804.

Clark spent most of that winter selecting and training members of the expedition and supervising the repair and modification of the three crafts that would take the expedition up the Missouri River. Lewis spent most of his time in St. Louis, making contacts, studying maps, gathering information, interviewing men who had been up the Missouri, and purchasing a seemingly endless amount of supplies and equipment.

The red-haired captain, Clark, had his hands full. Despite the occasional hard work, the men were bored. They loafed, got drunk, fought each other, angered the local farmers by stealing livestock, and failed to follow military protocol. Men refused to accept Sergeant Ordway's authority in the captains' absence. Court-martials for insubordination and drunkenness became common. Clark organized foot races and shooting matches, good training for the coming journey, to raise the men's spirits. The men parched corn, made sugar, found a bee tree and collected honey, gambled, and drank.

They dragged the boats from the water, initially to keep them from grounding in Wood River when water levels dropped, but later to prevent their being damaged by ice flows. Even the Mississippi might freeze, and it would surely run with ice that might damage the boats. Small quiet-water tributaries like Wood River would certainly freeze.

After the men constructed huts to shelter themselves from the weather, Clark set them to work on the boats, building two rows of lockers for storage on the keelboat, the closed covers serving as a walkway for poling the heavy craft. They built eleven rowing benches and attached eleven sets of blocks with thole pins to the gunnels.

How did the rowers attach the oars to the thole pins? No one knows. I can only make an educated guess: they tied them in with rope or rawhide. They used what they brought with them or what they found on the river, or they did without. Lewis's iron boat failed because they did not bring proper caulking material along and they could find none of what they needed (pine pitch) in the area.

While the men worked on the keelboat, repaired two pirogues, and rigged all the crafts with sails and rudders, Clark spent much of the winter calculating the time and distances of the expedition's move up the Missouri. He also considered the carrying capacity and manpower needs of the expedition: how many boats would be required? how many men to power them? how far could they travel in a day? how long would the trip take them? All of these questions were closely contemplated as Lewis and Clark planned and communicated across the Mississippi.

In the spring, once the ice melted, they launched the crafts to make training runs, testing both keelboat and pirogues. They ferried the captains and visiting dignitaries across the river to and from St. Louis in the pirogues. They watched Missouri River traffic. The party received visitors in canoes and pirogues passing on the Mississippi. Their visitors provided useful information, exotic foods, and news of the outside world. Such visits relieved the boredom of their isolation.

Clark's spring duties included loading the accumulated equipment and provisions onto the three boats. Supplies kept arriving: barrels of flour and salt pork, hog lard and beans, coffee and soap, candles and wicks, trade goods and Indian gifts, assorted camp equipage, vital tools, clothing, material for tents, awnings, and mosquito netting.

As spring progressed, though they still had frosty mornings, they saw more boats on the river. On April 15, two boats under sail passed by head-

The men at Camp Wood built lockers on the keelboat to haul equipment and supplies. The closed locker lids formed a catwalk for poling the craft; open, they formed a defensive breastwork and were once used to deflect high waves.

ing up the Mississippi. Spanish trader Manuel Lisa, who knew the river, visited (some of the men later joined his venture). They divided the cargo and packed the crafts to equalize the loads. On May 8, after a trial run in the keelboat, manned with twenty oars, they found the bow too heavily loaded and rearranged the load. Lewis remained in St. Louis buying supplies, gathering information, and partying. On May 14, 1804, the expedition left Camp Wood, crossed the Mississippi, and headed up the Missouri. The waiting was over; they were on their way at last.

FORT MANDAN. The expedition spent their second winter near Mandan and Hidatsa villages on the upper Missouri River near the mouth of Knife River in present-day North Dakota. They built a small triangular fort near the riverbank and named it Fort Mandan. The river froze before they pulled the boats from the water, locking the crafts into the ice for the winter. Concerned about what the spring break-up might do to the boats, Lewis and Clark had the men spend several days in late winter trying to free the crafts, a cold frustrating job because the river had frozen in several layers. Each time they broke through a layer, water would well up from below and refreeze, locking the crafts in even tighter.

Temperatures dropped so severely that the party did not need the pirogues to ferry hunters or visiting chiefs across the river: they could—and did—walk right across the river ice to visit and hunt. Ice bridges across the frozen Missouri expanded the expedition's hunting range and gave the captains access to Indian villages on the opposite shore where they gathered information from both tribes.

Clark kept a close watch on the river, both in the fall, when it began to run with ice and then freeze up, and again in the spring, when the river thawed and an ice gorge ripped down the Missouri, followed by drowned buffalo that had fallen through the ice over the winter. Local tribes feasted on the dead buffalo, too tainted for expedition members to tolerate. That winter the men began to eat, even relish, dog meat. It became a staple item in their diet west of the Continental Divide. Lewis liked it; Clark could not tolerate it.

An ice gorge occurs when river ice breaks up in the spring—or during a winter chinook (warm south wind)—and jams, damming the river. As the river rises behind this ice-dam, water pressure building up exerts pressure on the dam. Water may overflow the dam and refreeze, raising the dam level, or simply break through. In either case, sooner or later a mass of cold water and jagged ice surges down the river, scouring the riparian environment, scarring trees, gouging banks, and generally raising hell with the landscape along the river. Running the Middle Fork of the Salmon in central Idaho the first week of May, 1973, I found evidence of a recent ice gorge that remained all summer. The Yellowstone River in Montana suffers ice gorges, flooding riverside homes, the result of unpredictable ice dams appearing overnight.

At Fort Mandan, the men of the expedition kept busy, building their huts, hunting to enhance their meat supply, and cutting firewood to combat the numbing cold. The blacksmiths spent their time making battle-axes for Mandan warriors (so much for making peace among the tribes), trading their products for corn, dried squash, and beans, food to vary their diet. The men found Mandan women from whom they acquired venereal diseases, a perpetual problem for the expedition men. (The captains treated the venereal diseases and other ailments with compounds of mercury. One method of verifying Lewis and Clark campsites is finding traces of mercury in the expedition latrines.)

The captains gathered information from Indians, from French and British traders and trappers living with the tribes, and from a steady stream of traders visiting the Indian villages. They hired the French Canadian, Toussaint Charbonneau, who spoke French and several Indian languages, as an interpreter. It was here that his young Lemhi Shoshone wife, Sacagawea, became a valuable member of the party, not only for her interpreting skills with her people but also as a peace symbol. No war party traveled with a woman and child. Before the winter ended, she gave birth to their son, who accompanied the party.

Late that winter the captains sent out a party to build canoes, at first only four, but eventually six dugouts. They found cottonwood trees big enough for canoes several miles upstream and a mile and a half from the river. The keelboat, no longer needed and with too deep a draft to continue upriver, would return to St. Louis with documents and specimens collected by the expedition on its way up the Missouri the previous year. The expedition would continue upstream toward the Missouri headwaters in the two pirogues and six dugout canoes.

On April 7, 1805, the keelboat left for St. Louis as the permanent party started up the Missouri. The French rivermen, all but Cruzatte and Labiche, were gone. It was up to the American soldiers to get the job done. A woman, a baby, and thirty-two men and a dog left Fort Mandan for the Pacific.

As they departed Fort Mandan, Lewis wrote, "This little fleet altho' not quite so rispectable as those of Columbus or Capt. Cook were still viewed by us with as much pleasure as those deservedly famed adventurers ever beheld theirs; and I dare say with quite as much anxiety for their safety and preservation. we are now about to penetrate a country at least two thousand miles in width, on which the foot of civilized man has never trodden; the good or evil it had in store for us was for experiment yet to determine, and these little vessels contained every article by which we were to expect to subsist or defend ourselves."[11] Lewis's words reflect his sense of history and his concern as well as his excitement.

As a river-running historian, I am compelled to mention Major John Wesley Powell's journal entry as he and his men, camped at the mouth of the Little Colorado, prepared to enter the Grand Canyon sixty-five years later:

> *We are now ready to start on our way down the Great Unknown. Our boats, tied to a common stake, chafe each other as they are tossed by the fretful river. . . . We have an unknown distance yet to run, an unknown river yet to explore. What falls there are, we know not; what rocks beset the channels, we know not; what walls rise over the river, we know not.*[12]

Lewis and Clark led their party through a relatively well-known, well-peopled area. Powell and his men ventured into true wilderness, unknown and unpopulated. From the perspective of civilization, both parties traveled unexplored territory. Their leaders entered unexplored worlds with trepidation and a sense of history. They were fully aware of the importance of their respective ventures and their roles.

FORT CLATSOP. Although the expedition reached the Pacific in the middle of November, it didn't settle into winter camp until December 7. The explorers had traveled down the north side of the Columbia, sustaining the brunt of southwestern winds and ocean swells at the river's wide mouth. Weather conditions, high waves, and tidal quirks pinned them down for weeks as they struggled to survive in the rain and wind at the river's mouth. Discouraged by their exploration of the north shore, they retreated several miles upstream to a narrower part of the river protected by a series of islands and crossed to the south shore.

On the south side of the Columbia they found a suitable campsite a few miles up a tributary stream, the Netul River to local Indians, now known as the Lewis and Clark River. On high ground some two hundred yards from this tidal river they built their winter quarters and named it Fort Clatsop for the local Indian tribe, whose friendly members visited frequently, bringing gifts of food and pelts and hats to trade.

The expedition spent almost four months at Fort Clatsop. It rained nearly every day. Elk were plentiful, but with the weather so relatively warm, meat spoiled before they could use it or cure it. The hides became clothes for the men, many of whom were nearly naked; their clothing had

Expedition members built Fort Clatsop on the Netul (now Lewis
and Clark) River, seen here beyond a replica of an Indian burial
canoe on the hill above Astoria, Oregon.

worn out and rotted off their bodies in the constant rain. The winter at
Fort Clatsop was not cold, just wet and miserable.

Their river crafts helped sustain them. Nearly every day parties in canoes went out to hunt or to trade for food. The high tide took an occasional
canoe before expedition members learned to pull their crafts farther onto
the shore at their canoe landing and to tie them securely. They purchased
a second Indian canoe for their return up the Columbia and stole a third
when the owner refused to sell for what the captains offered. The expedition was short of trade items.

The Indians visited nearly every day with food to trade including sturgeon and candlefish, roots and berries, a variety of pelts and conical rain
hats. Once the expedition acquired a supply of whale meat and oil from a
blue whale the Indians had found grounded on a beach near the expedition's salt works. By mid-March the expedition had had enough rain to last
a lifetime. Anxious to head home, they left Fort Clatsop as spring arrived
and began their struggle up the mighty river toward the distant Divide.

CAMP CHOPUNNISH. By leaving the rainy coastal area earlier than planned,
the expedition tried to jump the season, but it was still winter in the Bit-

Fort Clatsop near the mouth of the Columbia River served as the
expedition's winter quarters.

terroots: deep snow prevented their crossing the mountains, delaying
them for nearly a month in a "spring" camp at what is now called Camp
Chopunnish on the Clearwater River in Nez Perce country, land of the
friendly tribe that had cared for their horses over the winter.

Since their camp on the Clearwater isolated them from the Nez Perce
people with whom they traded for food, they built another canoe for ferrying men and meat, trade goods and roots, but they used it for only a few
days before leaving for the Bitterroots, happy to be on their way home.

Even when they no longer traveled the rivers, when they settled into
these temporary winter quarters and their brief spring camp, the men used
the rivers to hunt and to fish, to ferry meat and building materials to camp,
to trade with local Indians, and to explore the region and expand their
knowledge. Whenever they were forced to wait, the expedition members
made the most of it, resting and catching up with their journal writing; tan-
ning hides and making clothes and moccasins; repairing boats and making oars, paddles, and poles; gathering information, stockpiling food, and
preparing for the next leg of the journey. Whenever they played the waiting game, the expedition took advantage of the respite and used it to their
advantage.

Conclusion

THE IMPACT OF THE
LEWIS AND CLARK EXPEDITION

What impact did the Lewis and Clark expedition have? What did they discover? What did the Corps of Discovery accomplish? What lessons did they learn or fail to learn? We can only tickle the edges of these questions in this brief conclusion.

Gary Moulton summarizes Jefferson's goals for the expedition: "The captains were to open a highway for the American fur trade, to win over the Indians from Spanish or British influence, and to lay the foundation for what Jefferson hoped would be a carefully regulated trade and intercourse with the Indians that would avoid some of the evils of unrestrained competition and interracial conflict so common in American experience." They were also "to observe and record the whole range of natural history and ethnology of the area and the possible resources for future settlers,"[1] a large order for the two captains, whose responsibilities also included hauling a heavily loaded keelboat and two large pirogues up the Missouri, building new boats whenever and wherever they needed them, and keeping the Corps of Discovery alive and well, active and productive during twenty-eight months in the wilderness.

Was the expedition successful? It failed to find that easy water route for commerce across the continent, but none existed. It failed to foster a lasting peace among the Indian tribes they met along their route. It failed to favorably impress the more powerful tribes (Teton Sioux, Blackfeet). It failed to stop interracial conflict among the Indians along the Columbia and Missouri Rivers, perhaps even within the Corps of Discovery itself though the permanent party included a Negro, an Indian, several mixed-bloods. There seems to have been relatively little intercourse between the permanent party and the French-Canadian crew of the red pirogue. They were rarely mentioned in the journals, but none of the writers traveled in the red pirogue.

Did Jefferson expect too much of the expedition? He had been operating without vital information. He lacked an understanding of the lay of the land and the nature of its indigenous peoples. Did he hold unrealistic expectations? At one point in the evolution of his thinking about "the Indian problem," he planned to keep American settlers out of the western United States, to reserve lands west of the Mississippi for the Indians, an idea that seems naive, given the American penchant for moving west and the Indians' resistance to losing their land and becoming farmers.

In his preface to the new Red River Books edition of *Southern Counterpart to Lewis and Clark: The Freeman and Custis Expedition of 1806*, Dan Flores writes that "western history probably wouldn't have turned out much differently," had the expedition been turned back by Spanish attempts to stop it, because "traders carrying American goods (and even flags) still intruded themselves among the Indian tribes in the Southwest,"[2] even after the Freeman and Custis expedition of 1806 had been stopped on the Red River. Flores suggests that Lewis and Clark didn't so much open the West as verify it, that the trappers and traders were already flooding the West when the expedition went up the Missouri. Evidence of such activity lies in the journals themselves.

Despite the obvious failures of the Lewis and Clark expedition, it had its successes. It returned with the loss of only one man and with new knowledge about the land and its people. The captains, serving as both ethnologists and naturalists, brought back useful information about Indian culture and natural history. They laid a foundation for trade with the Indians, helped wrest control of trade from the Spanish and British, and established an American foothold in the Northwest.

Even though they traveled largely by river, Lewis and Clark, and we as their literary descendents, learned a great deal about the land along the northern tier of what would become the western United States. Within five years of the expedition's return, entrepreneurs from the United States would establish trading posts on the Yellowstone and upper Missouri, even west of the Continental Divide near the headwaters of the Snake and at the mouth of the Columbia. Within sixty years steamboats were traveling up the Missouri as far as the mouth of the Marias River to serve the rapidly expanding American population.

As to the indigenous people of the area, the expedition may have opened trade with various tribes, but it began to close Indian options and to end their domination of much of North America. It resulted in disruption and destruction of tribal life in less than a century, the decimation of native populations, and the demise of Indian culture. What opened the West to "Americans," closed the West to native people. The people who most helped the expedition were soon wiped out by disease and driven off their land by Jefferson's agrarian society.

Impact on the Landscape

As an extension of the lessons Jefferson learned from Lewis and Clark, we have discovered that the landscape they crossed had been created and carved by the rivers they traveled, had been ordered and organized in natural patterns by the courses of those rivers. They saw the land from the rivers, experienced it from the riparian habitat. Although they traveled far from the major rivers on overland treks, the lands they crossed were drained by a network of small streams that dictated their route and flowed into those rivers.

The physical laws that govern the flow of water still control that landscape, despite the many dams that have altered its appearance and its character. Water still flows downhill and downstream, eroding the land and depositing silt along the rivers and in their reservoirs. Rivers still flood, still eat away the land despite modern dams and dikes. They still deposit sand and silt in the wake of their floods to fill irrigation ditches and reservoirs and to block river channels.

The laws of nature still dominate the region, largely because it is so vast and so dry, a fact not lost on the perceptive captains, and because much of it has been set aside for protection as wild and scenic rivers, national parks and monuments, and wilderness.

The Wild and Scenic Rivers Act, which became law in 1968, established a national policy protecting certain rivers, along with their adjacent lands, "in their free-flowing condition to protect the water quality of such rivers and to fulfill other vital national conservation purposes . . . for the benefit and enjoyment of present and future generations." To qualify, a

The top of Beacon Rock appears in the center, above and beyond
Bonneville Dam, the farthest downstream dam and the first built
on the lower Columbia to begin the transformation of the river
into a series of impoundments.

river must possess "outstandingly remarkable scenic, recreational, geo-
logic, fish and wildlife, historic, cultural, of other similar values."[3]

Much of the expedition's river route has become part of the National
Wild and Scenic Rivers System: long segments of the Missouri, Clear-
water, and Snake; portions of the Salmon, which Clark explored; several
Ohio and numerous Columbia River tributaries; and the Clark Fork of the
Yellowstone (but to date, none of the Yellowstone itself).

Many of these headwater streams begin in national forests and national
parks, much of it in designated wilderness areas. Spectacular lands along
the wild and scenic stretch of the upper Missouri that so fascinated the expedition journalists, the White Cliffs area and the Missouri Breaks, have
recently become a national monument. The expedition's route across the
Bitterroot Mountains remains nearly as wild and primitive as it was two
hundred years ago.

Today, as we fly over that same landscape, drive its modern highways or
ride the railroads—most of which follow the rivers as the expedition did—
float its rivers for recreation, ride horseback or hike trails along its wilder

A tugboat pushes a pair of barges on the still waters of a Columbia
River reservoir on the Lewis and Clark route.

portions, we can experience the wonder of its magnitude, its vast open
spaces, its spectacular vistas and wild charm.

Still the landscape has been altered forever.

Vast stretches of the rivers Lewis and Clark traveled—the Missouri,
Snake, and Columbia—are now dammed into strings of dead water reservoirs often called "lakes." All lakes by their very nature are dying, filling
with loess, evaporates, and eroded sediments; with organic wastes, toxic
chemicals, and the debris of modern civilization. At taxpayer expense we
have traded free-flowing rivers for dying reservoirs, subsidizing agribusiness, barge traffic, and the aluminum industry in a gross example of corporate welfare.

These rivers, now dammed and dredged, no longer live as the Corps
of Discovery experienced them. Their impoundments have separated Indian tribes and farm families from one another along the middle Missouri;
they have inundated rich farmlands and vital winter wildlife habitat; they
have decimated salmon and steelhead populations; and they have flooded
vast wetlands and altered natural processes. The Corps of Discovery has
been supplanted by the Corps of Engineers.

Four dams now block the flow of the Columbia, slowing annual
salmon migrations and killing tens of thousands of salmon and
steelhead smolt on their way to ocean pastures.

Reservoirs have permanently inundated thousands of acres in the
name of flood control, power production, irrigation, and recreation, yet
floods still occur in ever-greater magnitude and frequency because modern society seems no longer to respect rivers. Rampant development creates greater runoff, and rivers have been diked too tightly, leaving them no
room to roam in their natural flow to the sea. The very landscape has been
altered, floodplains violated, and weather patterns changed.

Lewis and Clark would not recognize the landscape through which
they traveled or the rivers that served them so well. While they helped
open the West to trade and commerce in their quest for the Northwest
Passage, we have created our own northwest passage by turning Lewiston,
Idaho, and Clarkston, Washington, cities named for the explorers, into seaports hundreds of miles from the ocean, by damming the Columbia and
Snake. We have destroyed the essence of the Great Falls of the Missouri
by converting them to the utilitarian. As Wallace Stegner once wrote about
the Glen Canyon reservoir, known as Lake Powell, "In gaining the lovely
and the usable, we have given up the incomparable."[4]

Impact on Native Peoples

When Lewis and Clark crossed the continent, they found a rich land teeming with wildlife, wild fruits and berries, and unique plants. They also found the land inhabited by numerous native peoples, perhaps more than anyone imagined. The expedition members learned that the "wilderness" through which they traveled was already well populated with indigenous people who had been there for generations and were making a good living off buffalo and salmon and camas roots.

In retrospect we see that it took "civilized" humankind a little more than a century to totally wipe out the passenger pigeon, which Lewis observed flying across the Ohio River the fall of 1803 (the last one died in a Cincinnati zoo in 1914). It took humankind less than a century to reduce the vast herds of buffalo (bison) to near extinction and less than two centuries to decimate the salmon of the Columbia River basin, all living creatures that supported Native Americans and members of the expedition.

In the thirty years since I began running the Middle Fork of the Salmon River in central Idaho, one of the instant-eight wild rivers and a major tributary of the Snake, salmon have all but disappeared. In 1972 they thrilled us with their spectacular leaps through the cold clear water of Dagger Falls while we waited to launch our rafts below. In the deep pool at the mouth of Pistol Creek we watched the salmon preparing to run the rapids upstream and saw fishermen catch them.

Few salmon appear at Dagger Falls today and there are even fewer fishermen; the salmon fishing season in much of Idaho has been closed for years. For all practical purposes, the Salmon River and its numerous once-productive tributaries are virtually devoid of the fish that gave the river its name, species that once fed the Lewis and Clark expedition and native people.

In that same year Dworshak Dam on the North Fork of the Clearwater River closed its gates, blocking forever from the ocean pastures the spawning waters of the greatest steelhead run in North America (you can see the dam across the Clearwater River from the Lewis and Clark Canoe Camp). That spring I witnessed the last log run down

The Great Falls of the Missouri are no longer great. All of the major
drops have been relegated to a reservoir-release regime that
often reduces the flow to a trickle.

*the North Fork. That summer steelhead still ran in the Imnaha River,
a tributary of the Snake in Hells Canyon. Now they too have all but
disappeared along with the sturgeon, another native species that
helped feed the expedition members and native people, one that responds negatively to dams.*

What opened the West to American traders and trappers irrevocably altered the lives of every member of every Indian tribe through whose territory the expedition passed. It changed the balance of power in the region, brought decimating diseases to the tribes, and altered the tribes'
ways of life. Instead of spending their efforts providing food and clothing
for their families, they engaged in hunting and trapping to trade furs, buffalo robes, and meat to the white man for guns and powder, iron and lead,
whiskey and foofaraw.

The Corps of Discovery found a healthy landscape that supported
many tribes of indigenous people, a landscape that may have seemed like
wilderness to the American explorers but was home to thousands of Na-

tive Americans. Without those native people who provided food, horses, dogs (as food), information, and expertise, the expedition would have accomplished little. Tribes fed them and individuals led them across the Continental Divide and through the mountains.

Certainly the expedition learned that the residents of the region lived well off the land and its waters, that they knew the land and its natural resources. Journal writers occasionally described the indigenous people in negative terms, but they depended on the Indians numerous times in various situations: Indians caught their wayward canoes and horses, showed them the portage routes, taught them the burn and chip method of hollowing canoes, returned lost property, gave them food and horses, and traded them horses that enabled the expedition to cross the mountains and to hunt for the wildlife that fed them.

Most tribes befriended the expedition; others resisted their passage. Native Americans have reveled in their association with the expedition. Nonetheless, a negative undercurrent, like the subtle movement of conflicting currents in the great rivers they traveled, disturbs the surface. A level of resentment eddies through Native American communities reflecting treatment of their ancestors by the expedition and later generations of white men. It reflects the demise of Indian culture as a result of the expedition. Lewis and Clark are no more popular in some Indian communities than Christopher Columbus.

Impact on Natural History

How wild was the wilderness through which the expedition traveled and explored? It was full of people, but it was full of wildlife as well, much of it previously unknown in the United States, certainly unknown to science and the rest of the world. There were new plants, too, species never before described until Lewis and Clark saw them.[5] The captains described three hundred new species: 178 new plants, 122 new animal species.

The abundance of wildlife, meat on the hoof, led to exploitation of that resource that continues today throughout the world. Expedition hunters began to take only the best cuts of meat. They left animals in poor condition to rot where they fell, food for wolves, which they also killed and sometimes ate. They slaughtered creatures with little or no food value, birds that were mere curiosities like the California condor, white pelican, and bald eagle, all in the name of science or to feed hungry men.

Lewis wrote at one time that "we take only what is necessary to feed the crew," but before long, especially on the return trip, they often killed several buffalo for a single day's meal, taking only the tongue or other choice portions. Lewis and his nine men killed eleven buffalo on their return to the Great Falls of the Missouri for food and hides to build two skin boats. They lived off the land, using animal skins for trade and clothing when they had exhausted their supply. They killed dozens of elk and deer primarily for the hides. The animals were there for the taking, and they took all they could.

Pioneer naturalists, as Cutright termed them, Lewis and Clark both had plant and animal species named for them, Lewis's woodpecker, Clark's grebe, and Clark's nutcracker among the birds they first described. Several wildflowers carry the captains' names. *Lewisia rediviva*, or bitterroot, Montana's state flower, was first collected by Lewis in the Bitterroot Valley in 1806. Native people and mountain men used its root as a favorite food. The pink monkey-flower, *Mimulus lewisii*, and blue flax, *Linum lewisii*, were both named for Lewis; ragged robin, *Clarkia pulchella*, a wildflower also known as Clarkia, deerhorn, and pink-fairies, was initially found along the Clearwater River. (I first saw it on the Selway River, a founding source of the Clearwater). The cutthroat trout is also named for Clark *(Oncorhynchus clarki* and *Salmo clarki)*.

Lewis wrote long passages describing plants and animals. The expedition collected skins, skulls, and bones of many creatures; they even took a few alive and sent them back to President Jefferson. Lewis collected and pressed plants and took soil and mineral samples. Not as well versed in science as Lewis, Clark nonetheless did his best to collect and describe plants and animals they found along their way.

For all their efforts to bring back evidence of the new plant and animal species, important scientific knowledge, Lewis and Clark helped open the floodgates to the wholesale exploitation of those natural resources.

Impact on Natural Resources

Wildlife abounded along the expedition's route: thousands of buffalo, hundreds of elk (with a capital E in many of the journal entries), deer on every island, beaver wherever they found timber and many places they didn't. The "Myth of Superabundance" that Stewart Udall wrote about in

Clark's nutcracker *(Nucifraga columbiana)* was first described by
William Clark on August 2, 1805, near present-day Tendoy, Idaho.
It was later named for the explorer, who first identified it
as a new species.

The Quiet Crisis began with Lewis and Clark, so much wildlife that it could
never be exhausted, the buffalo-hunter mentality that still dominates
American thinking (should we drill for oil in the Arctic National Wildlife
Refuge in Alaska and ignore the wildlife?).

In a chapter titled "The Raid on Resources," Udall wrote, "A temper-
ate continent, rich in soils and minerals and forests and wildlife, enticed
men to think in terms of infinity rather than facts, and produced an over-
riding fallacy that was nearly our undoing—the Myth of Superabundance." Then, "According to the myth, our resources were inexhaustible.
It was an assumption that made wise management of the land and provi-
dent husbandry superfluous."[6] It still does.

Lewis and Clark brought back tales of unlimited wildlife, rich bottom-
land soils, vast forests, and minerals galore. No doubt other members of
the expedition spread the same tales by word of mouth. After the expedition, several members of the Corps of Discovery became beaver trappers
on the upper Missouri and its tributaries; they were among the first of the
mountain men, what Udall called "the White Indians." The expedition

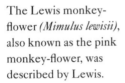

The Lewis monkey-
flower *(Mimulus lewisii)*,
also known as the pink
monkey-flower, was
described by Lewis.

led to a century of exploitation, of killing off that wildlife, of stripping the
land bare of its native vegetation, of cutting those forests and mining those
minerals. That profligate pattern continues.

Exploitation of resources, even human resources, grew out of Jeffer-
sonian philosophy, the primary reason Jefferson sent Lewis and Clark
across the continent. The president wanted to expand the nation, to develop commerce, to extend American influence. Exploitation of the new
world's vast resources was the name of the game. Not until those resources
became scarce did conservation emerge as a meaningful idea.

Udall addressed the mountain men's impact: "Their undisciplined
creed of reckless individualism became the code of those who later used a
higher technology to raid our resources systematically. The spiritual sons
of the mountain men were the next wave—the skin-and-scoot market
hunters, the cut-and-get-out lumbermen, the cattle barons whose herds

Lewis discovered *Clarkia pulchella*, commonly called ragged robin, on June 1, 1806, in the valley of the Clearwater River in Idaho, but it was named for Clark. This specimen I photographed on the nearby Selway River, a founding tributary of the Clearwater.

grazed the plains bare."[7] They were the forerunners of the sagebrush rebels and "wise use" advocates.

A flood of farmers followed, inundating the Great Plains, ripping open the prairie sod and the Willamette Valley of Oregon Territory, and cutting the forests to build farms. The Oregon Trail opened in the 1840s, a generation after the mountain men headed west; a generation later railroads crossed the continent, splitting the great buffalo population into a northern and southern herd and creating a market for the hides, tongues, tallow, meat, and finally the skulls and bones of the buffalo.

A major result of the Lewis and Clark expedition was to create the Myth of Superabundance and initiate the buffalo-hunter mentality. The expedition opened the West to exploitation and changed the nature of the West forever, but that exploitation ultimately led to the conservation movement that began a century after the expedition. It gained momentum as resources dwindled, species disappeared, and more people became aware of what they had lost.

Aldo Leopold wrote, in the introduction to *A Sand County Almanac,* "we abuse the land because we regard it as a commodity belonging to us. When we see land as a community to which we belong, we may begin to use it with love and respect."[8] As we move into the twenty-first century, we ignore this concept of a land ethic at our peril. Important environmental legislation, passed during the final third of the twentieth century, has recently been eroded to the detriment of the land and its people.

FOOTHOLD CONCEPT. Although the Lewis and Clark expedition did not settle any of the territory it explored, it established an American foothold in the West. Before the expedition returned, entrepreneurs were sending trading expeditions up the Missouri. In 1807 Manuel Lisa established a trading post where the Bighorn River flows into the Yellowstone; in 1811, as the Astorians headed west, Andrew Henry crossed the Continental Divide to build an outpost on the headwaters of the Snake River.

In 1822 Henry and William Ashley accelerated the mountain man movement, and the settlement of the West received its first real boost. The mountain men followed the rivers but didn't settle; they merely cleared the path for settlement. Two decades after Ashley and Henry ventured up the Missouri, the Oregon Trail opened, following rivers, and the flood of immigrants began to settle the West.

A generation later, as the Civil War ended, a second wave of settlers headed west onto the Great Plains, uprooting the indigenous people, stealing Indian lands, initiating the Indian wars, and settling the West, a delayed result of the Lewis and Clark expedition. With the buffalo gone and the Indians extirpated, European immigrants joined the flood. The America we know had begun to take form.

Impact on Personnel

More than sixty people participated directly in the Lewis and Clark expedition in one way or another. The two captains and members of the permanent party were joined by various interpreters and guides. The crew of the red pirogue, a necessary adjunct to expedition success, provided useful training in river expertise for members of the Corps of Discovery; they provided entertainment and interpretation and some degree of understanding the tribes along the rivers.

Most of the French boatmen disappeared from expedition records by the spring of 1805, but one (E. Cann) helped the Astorians establish Astoria. Several members of the expedition turned to trapping: Colter, Drouillard, Collins, Newman, Potts, Shields, and Weiser. For the few years of life left to him, Drouillard maintained close contact with Clark; the interpreter was killed by Blackfeet Indians near the Three Forks in 1810. John Collins joined William Ashley's trapping expedition to the upper Missouri (1822) and died in the battle with the Arikara in 1823.

Newman, one of the men expunged from the permanent party, trapped on the Missouri in the Dakotas for years; he was killed by the Yankton Sioux in the summer of 1838. Weiser joined Manuel Lisa's fur brigade to the Yellowstone and upper Missouri; he may have ventured into the Snake River drainage, for a tributary of the Snake in western Idaho as well as a town on that river seem to have been named for him.

Potts and Colter both became trappers on the upper Missouri. Potts was killed by the Blackfeet in the same encounter that led to Colter's miraculous escape. Shields, a relative of Daniel Boone, trapped briefly on the lower Missouri with Boone, then settled in Indiana, where he died. Charbonneau, too, continued to work for Clark who kept him employed as an interpreter for years. Sacagawea died at about twenty-four in 1812, just a few years after the expedition's return though the story of her living a long life among the Wyoming Shoshone persists.

Clark educated their son, Jean Baptiste (Pompey), who led an interesting life among several cultures: he lived in Germany, guided the Mormon Battalion and several important personages through the West, participated in the California gold rush, and died in 1866 at the age of sixty-one in southeastern Oregon.

Lewis became governor of the Louisiana Territory, a position to which he was poorly fitted. He could not seem to get involved in editing the expedition journals, and the many petty duties of his position discouraged him. He drank a great deal, got into debt, and depressed by his failures, committed suicide in 1809.

As Superintendent of Indian Affairs, Clark thrived and prospered. On the expedition, he had been closer to the Indians than Lewis, generally more tolerant and understanding. He continued to rework his map of the West, augmenting it with information from traders and trappers, among them several members of the expedition. He became a partner in a successful trading venture and lived until 1838. I often think of him as "the red-haired captain," a spiritual twin of Menelaus in *The Odyssey*.

Individual Indians the expedition members encountered gained prestige from their contact with the expedition—or lost it. Tribal memories have expanded the story of the Corps of Discovery, offering varied reactions to their contact with the expedition. Several individuals claim to be descendents of Lewis or Clark or York. With few exceptions the expedition probably impacted the people they met more profoundly than it impacted expedition members themselves. The captains both became famous and earned high positions as a result of their efforts, but most of the men simply disappeared from history.

George Shannon, the youngest member of the expedition, lost a leg in the battle with the Arikara when several expedition members under Sergeant Pryor attempted to return the Mandan chief Sheheke to his people. He didn't let that stop him: he studied and practiced law, and before his death in 1836, became a Missouri state senator.

Patrick Gass, elected sergeant by his peers when Sergeant Floyd died, was a skilled carpenter responsible for building the expedition's winter quarters at Fort Mandan and Fort Clatsop and for building most of the canoes. After the expedition, he stayed in the army through the War of 1812, lost an eye in an accident that led to his discharge, married at sixty and settled in West Virginia, where he died in 1870, the last known survivor of the Lewis and Clark expedition. Little is known about other members of the permanent party following the expedition, but they each played a role in an America drama.

Impact on American Culture

Some scholars believe that the Lewis and Clark journals had a catalytic impact on the emergence of American art and literature. The May, 1992, edition of *We Proceeded On* features an article by Arlen J. Large, "Literary Borrowings from Lewis and Clark,"[9] pointing out that Edgar Allan Poe and James Fenimore Cooper, among others, borrowed from the journals. While the Nicholas Biddle edition of the journals wasn't published until 1814, Patrick Gass's journal appeared in 1807 only a year after the expedition's return. Widely distributed and wildly popular, it was republished several times, both in America and abroad.

Even more popular were "Apocryphal" versions of the journals, almost totally fictitious and highly romanticized, which began to appear in 1809, according to James P. Hendrix.[10] In his article in the *Great Plains Quarterly*,[11] Hendrix made a strong case for the cultural importance of the journals. Hendrix joined Rod Nash, Alan Weltzien, and me on a Western Literature Association panel the fall of 2001 discussing the literary impacts of the Lewis and Clark expedition. The panel left little doubt as to the importance of the journals in the evolution of an American culture.

Hendrix's presentation at the Pennsylvania State University "Lewis and Clark: The Unheard Voices" conference in the fall of 2002, suggested that the journals helped turn America away from Europe to the American West, from European antecedents to wilder, untamed elements introduced as subject matter by expedition members.

Before the expedition, most American readers looked to Europe for literature. The first American writer taken seriously by the European literary community was Washington Irving, who spent many years living and writing in Europe, but upon his return to America in 1832, he wrote increasingly about the American West, often drawing upon the journals, which first gave shape and scope to the West in the minds of readers. Earlier (1820s), James Fenimore Cooper's Leatherstocking Tales were set against an American landscape that reflects the journals.

Henry David Thoreau, in an essay called "Walking," found the West the land of the future: "Eastward I go only by force, but westward I go free," he wrote. "We go eastward to realize history and study the works of art and literature, retracing the steps of the race; we go westward as into the future, with a spirit of enterprise and adventure."[12] Thoreau's view of the West quite likely grew out a familiarity with the journals.

Certainly the novel of the early mountain men by A. B. Guthrie, Jr., *The Big Sky* (1947) draws heavily on the Lewis and Clark expedition as do modern fictional works such as Will Henry's *The Gates of the Mountains* (1963), Winfred Blevins's *Charbonneau: Man of Two Dreams* (1975, 1985), Anna Lee Waldo's *Sacajawea* (1978), and James Alexander Thom's *From Sea to Shining Sea* (1984) and *Sign Talker* (2001).

Numerous artists from George Catlin and Karl Bodmer to Charles M. Russell, Olaf Seltzer, Michael Haynes, Charles Fritz, John F. Clymer, and Gary P. Miller have painted scenes from the expedition's experience. Bronze statues depicting expedition events appear along the route of the expedition, and the bicentennial of the expedition has generated increased interest in the story and Lewis and Clark memorabilia.

Impact on the Modern West

The West that Lewis and Clark knew has changed in the two hundred years since they passed through it. Gone are the vast herds of buffalo and

elk, the unfettered rivers, the clear skies and natural vistas, the Great Falls
of the Missouri. It continues to change as each generation of modern society places greater demands on the natural environment, as it builds in the
floodplain and on the ridges, as it dewaters streams and introduces exotic
species and toxic pollutants.

Today even the Yellowstone River has been diked to protect private
property. Diversions drain its waters and create hazards for boaters. Coal
seams that Lewis and Clark observed have been mined; riprap has been
dumped along the riverbank to "prevent erosion"; and the Missouri River
paddlefish has become endangered. The wildlife that fed the expedition
has been replaced by domestic livestock, but the fishing remains good, at
least east of the Great Divide. However, many of the fish species are introduced exotics, and whirling disease runs rampant in some watersheds
as does chronic wasting disease among members of the deer family.

The Yellowstone has long been a candidate for wild and scenic river
protection, which it badly needs. It hardly resembles the river Clark explored two hundred years ago, and it is deteriorating rapidly as uncontrolled and unplanned development increases. But hey, this is the West;
it's supposed to be uncontrolled and unplanned, isn't it? That's what the
sagebrush rebels and wise use advocates tell us.

While the Yellowstone floods naturally, human intrusions have altered
its flow and caused property-damaging floods. During the winter the river
freezes; running water breaks out from beneath the ice, then freezes, creating ice dams that back up the flow to flood adjacent lands in the floodplain. People who don't have common sense enough to build outside the
floodplain will sooner or later suffer the consequences—just as expedition
members did when they failed to scout rapids.

Spring snowmelt causes annual flooding, some years greater than others. When floods threaten to damage property, home owners expect the
same local authorities they pressured into letting them build in the floodplain to protect them from natural floods. They want the officials to save
them from their own folly, as Indians along the Columbia rescued members of the expedition and retrieved their canoes and baggage. They call
for flood-control dikes built at public expense, thereby losing the natural
amenities that led them to build in the first place.

Change is inevitable, and we can't blame Lewis and Clark for opening
a Pandora's box of modern problems. They had their orders, and they fol-

lowed them. They lived in different times, had different realities, a different perspective.

The Corps of Engineers on the Missouri is presently taking a great deal of heat from the general public for its environmental insensitivity and its pandering to special interests with powerful political allies, but the Corps rarely responds to the people who pay the bills, the American taxpayer, who ultimately paid the cost of the expedition in several ways.

The Corps of Engineers, with its perpetual big budget and little accountability, has done more than any other single agency to destroy the natural character of the Missouri River, the Snake and Columbia, to alter their essential character. For some that is a positive thing; for most, it is a negative.

Many of the Corps' structural answers to flood control have actually created more frequent floods and floods of greater severity, most certainly permanent flooding behind dams. The engineers do not allow the river to flow into its natural floodplain. Rivers need room to roam, space to flow into when snowmelt and runoff exceeds normal carrying capacity that has been limited by the Corps' concrete, stone, and steel structures.

In his superb book, *The Columbia: Sustaining a Modern Resource*, Tim Palmer addresses many of these issues. In his final chapter he writes, "The fate of the Columbia Basin, with all its water and land, depends on people becoming involved in the future. Without support for political candidates who work toward a positive vision of the future, the entire watershed will default to the people who seek only personal gain and short-term profit."[13] The same could be said for the Ohio, Mississippi, Missouri, and Yellowstone river basins.

When we begin to destroy natural systems and our historical perspective, we lose both our past and our future. By looking back on the Lewis and Clark expedition, perhaps we can regain a little of both.

DISTANCES THE
EXPEDITION TRAVELED

Heading West	MILES	BY LAND	BY RIVER	UPRIVER	DOWNRIVER
Down the Ohio	1,126	——	1,126	——	1,126
Up the Mississippi	184	——	184	184	——
Up the Missouri	3,096	——	3,096	3,096	——
Divide/Bitterroots	398	398	——	——	——
Down CSC[a]	640	——	——	——	640
TOTAL MILEAGE	5,444	398	5,046	3,280	1,766

[a]Clearwater/Snake/Columbia (from Canoe Camp to the Pacific Ocean)

Heading East	MILES	BY LAND	BY RIVER	UPRIVER	DOWNRIVER
Up the Columbia	268	——	268	268	——
Overland to TR[b]	394	394	——	——	——
TOTAL TO TR	662	394	268	268	——

[b]Traveler's Rest, where the expedition split into two parties.

Separate Travels	MILES	BY LAND	BY RIVER	UPRIVER	DOWNRIVER
LEWIS:					
to Great Falls	183	183	——	——	——
to explore Marias	280	280	——	——	——
LEWIS TOTAL	463	463	——	——	——
CLARK:					
to Canoe Cache	160	160	——	——	——
to the Yellowstone	48	48	——	——	——
along Yellowstone	115	115	——	——	——
down Yellowstone	636	——	636	——	636
CLARK TOTAL	959	323	636	——	636
ORDWAY BJM[c]	3,096	——	3,096	——	3,096

[c]Beaverhead/Jefferson/Missouri (Ordway led the canoe party back down river by the expedition's upriver route; the Lewis and Clark parties join him on the Missouri)

Total Distance	MILES	BY LAND	BY RIVER	UPRIVER	DOWNRIVER
Heading West Total	5,444	398	5,046	3,280	1,766
Heading East Total	5,180	1,180	4,000	268	3,732
GRAND TOTAL	10,624	1,578	9,046	3,548	5,498

These totals are based on figures from the journals of the Lewis and Clark expedition, especially from "Postexpeditionary Miscellany."[1]

The Lewis and Clark expedition traveled 10,624 total miles, 9,046 by river. They sailed, rowed, towed, poled, and paddled 3,548 miles of that distance upstream against the current; 5,498 miles, going downstream with the flow.

After the expedition, when Lewis and Clark recorded their trip mileage, they calculated the shortest route. For example, on Lewis's shortcut from Traveler's Rest to the Great Falls, he actually traveled 183 miles, but when he learned of a shorter route that would have cut twenty miles off that distance, he used the shorter distance. I have used the actual distance rather than the theoretical distance.

Another example: on the Yellowstone River, Clark gave the actual mileage his party traveled along the river on horseback (115) during the four days before they found trees big enough to build canoes; he also gave the river miles they did not travel (191)—the distance they would have traveled if they had been floating down the river.

In the book I use "more than 10,000 miles" for the total trip distance, and "more than 9,000 miles by river." I use figures beginning August 31, 1803, at Pittsburgh, Pennsylvania, where the keelboat was built, where Lewis began keeping his journal, and where the river voyage, in my view, actually started. It ended at St. Louis three years and three weeks and three days later on September 23, 1806 (keep in mind that the expedition encompassed a leap year).

Notes

Preface

1. Donald Jackson, ed., *Letters of the Lewis and Clark Expedition, with Related Documents, 1783–1854,* vol. 1, 61.
2. Jackson, *Letters,* vol. 1, 243.
3. William Kittredge, *Taking Care: Thoughts on Storytelling and Belief,* 13.
4. Bernard De Voto, ed., *The Journals of Lewis and Clark,* v.

Chapter 1: The Ways of Wind and Water

1. Gary Moulton, *The Journals of the Lewis and Clark Expedition,* vol. 4, 29.
2. Ibid.
3. Ibid.
4. Alan S. Kesselheim, *Threading the Currents: A Paddler's Passion for Water,* 231.
5. Moulton, *Journals,* vol. 2, 84.
6. Luna B. Leopold, *A View of the River,* 9.
7. Kesselheim, *Threading the Currents,* 213.
8. Daniel B. Botkin, *Our Natural History: The Lessons of Lewis and Clark.*
9. See *National Geographic,* April, 2002, 90–97.
10. Botkin, *Our Natural History,* 21.
11. Wendell Berry, from the *Long-Legged House:* "The Rise," in *Recollected Essays, 1965–1980,* 5.
12. Kesselheim, *Threading the Currents,* 139.

Chapter 2: The Travelers

1. Charles G. Clarke, *The Men of the Lewis and Clark Expedition.* Most of the information in chapter 2 comes from Clarke, and from Moulton.
2. Moulton, *Journals,* vol. 2, 510.

3. Clarke, *Men*, 38.

4. Ibid., 44.

5. Moulton, *Journals*, vol. 2, 517.

6. Clarke, *Men*, 53.

Chapter 3: The Benefits and Hazards of River Travel

1. Zadok Cramer, *The Navigator*, 16.

2. Cramer, *Navigator*, 17.

3. Moulton, *Journals*, vol. 8, 297.

4. James P. Ronda, *Finding the West: Explorations with Lewis and Clark*, 11.

5. Jackson, *Letters*, vol. 1, 137.

6. Moulton, *Journals*, vol. 4, 379.

7. Winfred Blevins, *Dictionary of the American West*, 34.

8. Moulton, *Journals*, vol. 2, 230.

9. Cramer, *Navigator*, 18.

10. Moulton, *Journals*, vol. 4, 209.

11. Moulton, *Journals*, vol. 11, 165.

12. Moulton, *Journals*, vol. 3, 112.

Chapter 4: The Crafts

1. Moulton, *Journals*, vol. 2, 162.

2. David Lavender, *The Way to the Western Sea: Lewis and Clark across the Continent*, 58; Richard C. Boss, "Keelboat, Pirogue, and Canoe: Vessels Used by the Lewis and Clark Corps of Discovery," *Nautical Research Journal* (June, 1993): 69.

3. Boss, "Keelboat, Pirogue, and Canoe," 81.

4. Dayton Duncan, *Out West: An American Journey*.

5. Moulton, *Journals*, vol. 2, 214.

6. Jackson, *Letters*, vol. 2, 534.

7. Boss, "Keelboat, Pirogue, and Canoe," 69.

8. Stephen E. Ambrose, *Undaunted Courage: Meriwether Lewis, Thomas Jefferson, and the Opening of the American West*, 105.

9. Arlen J. Large, "The Rocky Boat Ride of Lewis and Clark," *We Proceeded On* vol. 21, no. 1 (February, 1995): 18.

10. Boss, "Keelboat, Pirogue, and Canoe," 77.

11. Don Holm, "Westward with Lewis and Clark," in Western Writers of America, ed., *Water Trails West*.

12. See Moulton, *Journals*, vol. 2, 196.

13. Lavender, *Way to the Western Sea*, 63.

14. Moulton, *Journals*, vol. 3, 19.

15. Bob Saindon, "The White Pirogue of the Lewis and Clark Expedition," *Proceedings*, Eighth Annual Meeting, Lewis and Clark Trail Heritage Foundation, Inc., August 1976, 16.

16. Large, "Rocky Boat Ride," 18.

17. Moulton, *Journals*, vol. 3, 307.
18. Moulton, *Journals*, vol. 4, 300.
19. Ibid., 305.
20. Saindon, "White Pirogue of the Lewis and Clark Expedition," 15.
21. Moulton, *Journals*, vol. 3, 304.
22. Ibid., 311.
23. Moulton, *Journals*, vol. 4, 373.
24. Moulton, *Journals*, vol. 5, 233.
25. Ibid., 235.
26. Ibid., 248.
27. Moulton, *Journals*, vol. 8, 209.
28. Ibid., 217.
29. Ibid., 252.
30. Moulton, *Journals*, vol. 4, 369.
31. Moulton, *Journals*, vol. 8, 106.
32. Moulton, *Journals*, vol. 2, 270.
33. Moulton, *Journals*, vol. 4, 260–61.

Chapter 5: The Rivers They Traveled

1. Moulton, *Journals*, vol. 2, 65.
2. Ibid., 67.
3. Ibid., 84.
4. Ibid., 86.
5. Ibid., 112.
6. Ibid., 101.
7. Ibid.
8. Ibid., 131.
9. Stanley Vestal, *The Missouri*, 5.
10. Vestal, *Missouri*, 6.
11. John G. Neihardt, *The River and I*, 23–24.
12. Moulton, *Journals*, vol. 4, 225.
13. Hank Fischer and Carol Fischer, *Paddling Montana*, 129.
14. Moulton, *Journals*, vol. 4, 204.
15. Ibid., 225.
16. Moulton, *Journals*, vol. 5, 43.
17. Ibid., 53.
18. Ibid., 248.
19. Ibid., 248–49.
20. Moulton, *Journals*, vol. 7, 308.
21. Moulton, *Journals*, vol. 9, 320.
22. Moulton, *Journals*, vol. 6, 48.
23. Robert Cantwell, *The Hidden Northwest*, 27–28.
24. Bob Saindon, "The 'Unhappy Affair' on Two Medicine River," *We Proceeded On* vol. 28, no. 3 (August, 2002): 14–15.

25. Moulton, *Journals*, vol. 8, 134.

26. Ibid., 134–35.

27. Fischer and Fischer, *Paddling Montana*, 184–88.

Chapter 6: Traveling Upstream and Down

1. Donald Jackson, *Thomas Jefferson and the Rocky Mountains*, 163.

2. Moulton, *Journals*, vol. 2, 227.

3. Moulton, *Journals*, vol. 11, 1.

4. Moulton, *Journals*, vol. 9, 6.

5. Moulton, *Journals*, vol. 2, 254.

6. Moulton, *Journals*, vol. 3, 128.

7. Holm, "Westward with Lewis and Clark," 70.

8. Moulton, *Journals*, vol. 4, 152.

9. Jackson, *Letters*, vol. 2, 534.

10. Moulton, *Journals*, vol. 2, 163.

11. Moulton, *Journals*, vol. 4, 403.

12. See Ralph K. Andrist, *Steamboats on the Mississippi*, 25–26.

13. Moulton *Journals*, vol. 4, 420.

14. Ibid., 423.

15. Moulton, *Journals*, vol. 2, 355.

16. Moulton, *Journals*, vol. 4, 158.

17. See Moulton, *Journals*, vol. 6, 152.

18. Ibid., 40.

19. Robert E. Hartley, *Lewis and Clark in the Illinois Country: The Little-Told Story*, 52–57.

20. Moulton, *Journals*, vol. 5, 265.

21. Ibid., 266.

22. Ibid., 268.

23. Moulton, *Journals*, vol. 9, 335.

24. Moulton, *Journals*, vol. 8, 138.

Chapter 7: River Incidents

1. Moulton, *Journals*, vol. 9, 147–48.

2. Ibid., 148.

3. Moulton, *Journals*, vol. 4, 154.

4. Ibid.

5. Ibid., 152.

6. Ibid., 29.

7. Ibid., 341.

8. Ibid., 342–43.

9. Moulton, *Journals*, vol. 5, 266.

10. Moulton, *Journals*, vol. 11, 340–41.

11. Ibid., 341–42.

12. Moulton, *Journals*, vol. 10, 151.

13. Moulton, *Journals*, vol. 5, 271–72.

14. Moulton, *Journals*, vol. 10, 155.

15. Moulton, *Journals*, vol. 11, 352.

16. Moulton, *Journals*, vol. 5, 326.

17. Ibid., 327.

18. Ibid.

19. Moulton, *Journals*, vol. 9, 345.

20. Moulton, *Journals*, vol. 8, 83.

21. Ibid., 83, 85.

22. Ibid., 175.

23. Ibid., 177–78.

24. Ibid., 178.

25. Moulton, *Journals*, vol. 9, 335.

26. James P. Ronda, *Lewis and Clark among the Indians*, 30.

27. Ronda, *Indians*, 40.

28. Moulton, *Journals*, vol. 2, 231.

29. Ibid., 229.

30. Moulton, *Journals*, vol. 2, 250.

31. Ibid., 289.

32. Ibid., 328.

33. Moulton, *Journals*, vol. 4, 111.

34. Ibid., 225.

Chapter 8: Off the River

1. Moulton, *Journals*, vol. 4, 369.

2. Moulton, *Journals*, vol. 5, 210.

3. Ibid., 211, n3. See also Moulton, *Journals*, vol. 11, 319.

4. Moulton, *Journals*, vol. 5, 213–14.

5. Ibid., 229.

6. Moulton, *Journals*, vol. 7, 160.

7. Ibid., 206.

8. Moulton, *Journals*, vol. 8, 7.

9. Ibid., 31.

10. Ibid., 53.

11. Moulton, *Journals*, vol. 4, 9.

12. John Wesley Powell, *The Exploration of the Colorado River and Its Canyons*, 47.

Conclusion: The Impact of the Lewis and Clark Expedition

1. Moulton, *Journals*, vol. 2, 5.

2. Dan L. Flores, ed., *Southern Counterpart to Lewis and Clark: The Freeman and Custis Expedition of 1806*, xvi.

3. *The Wild and Scenic Rivers Act*, Public Law 90–542, 16 U.S.C. 1271–1287, October 2, 1968, 1.

4. Wallace Stegner, *The Sound of Mountain Waters*, 128.

5. For a definitive look at the captains as naturalists, see Paul Russell Cutright's *Lewis and Clark: Pioneer Naturalists*.

6. Stewart Udall, *The Quiet Crisis*, 66.

7. Ibid., 48–49.

8. Aldo Leopold, *A Sand County Almanac*, viii.

9. Arlen J. Large, "Literary Borrowings from Lewis and Clark," *We Proceeded On* vol. 18, no. 2 (May, 1992): 12–19.

10. James P. Hendrix, Jr., paper presented at the conference "Lewis and Clark: The Unheard Voices," November 15, 2002, Pennsylvania State University.

11. James P. Hendrix, Jr., "A New Vision Of America: Lewis and Clark and the Emergence of the American Imagination," *Great Plains Quarterly* vol. 21, no. 3 (summer, 2001): 211–32.

12. Henry David Thoreau, "Walking," *Collected Essays and Poems*, 234.

13. Tim Palmer, *The Columbia: Sustaining a Modern Resource*, 131.

Appendix

1. Moulton, *Journals*, vol. 8, 376–94.

Bibliography

Allen, John Logan. *Passage through the Garden: Lewis and Clark and the Image of the American Northwest.* Urbana: University of Illinois Press, 1975; Mineola, N.Y.: Dover, 1991.

Ambrose, Stephen E. *Undaunted Courage: Meriwether Lewis, Thomas Jefferson, and the Opening of the American West.* New York: Simon & Schuster, 1996.

American Heritage Book of Great Adventures of the Old West. New York: American Heritage Press, 1969.

Andrist, Ralph K. *Steamboats on the Mississippi.* New York: American Heritage Publishing Company, 1962.

Bakeless, John. *The Eyes of Discovery.* New York: J. B. Lippincott, 1950.

———. *The Journals of Lewis and Clark.* New York: Mentor Books, 1964.

———. *Lewis and Clark: Partners in Discovery.* New York: William Morrow, 1947.

Baldwin, Leland D. *The Keelboat Age on Western Waters.* 1941; Pittsburgh: University of Pittsburgh Press, 1980.

Bartlett, Richard, ed. *Rolling Rivers: An Encyclopedia of America's Rivers.* New York: McGraw Hill, 1984.

Berry, Wendell. *Recollected Essays, 1965–1980.* San Francisco: North Point Press, 1981.

Blevins, Winfred. *Dictionary of the American West.* New York: Facts On File, 1993.

Boss, Richard C. "Keelboat, Pirogue, and Canoe: Vessels Used by the Lewis and Clark Corps of Discovery." *Nautical Research Journal* (June, 1993).

Botkin, Daniel B. *Our Natural History: The Lessons of Lewis and Clark.* New York: Berkley Publishing Group, 1996.

———. *Passage of Discovery.* New York: Berkley Publishing Group, 1999.

Cantwell, Robert. *The Hidden Northwest.* Philadelphia: J. B. Lippincott, 1972.

Chenoweth, Bob. "Dugout Canoes and Lewis and Clark's Journey to the Pacific." NAI 2002 Conference, February 23, 2002, unpublished.

Chittenden, Hiram Martin. *The American Fur Trade of the Far West.* 2 vols. Lincoln: University of Nebraska Press, 1986.

Clarke, Charles G. *The Men of the Lewis and Clark Expedition.* Lincoln: University of Nebraska Press, 2002.

Cody, Robin. *Voyage of a Summer Sun.* New York: Alfred A. Knopf, 1995.

Coues, Elliot, ed. *The History of the Lewis and Clark Expedition.* 3 vols. 1893, Francis P. Harper. Reprint, New York: Dover, 1987.

Cramer, Zadok. *The Navigator.* Pittsburgh, 1808.

Cutright, Russell Paul. *A History of the Lewis and Clark Journals.* Urbana: University of Illinois Press, 1976.

———. *Lewis and Clark: Pioneering Naturalists.* Urbana: University of Illinois Press, 1969; Lincoln: University of Nebraska Press, 1989.

De Voto, Bernard. *Across the Wide Missouri.* Boston: Houghton Mifflin, 1947.

———. *The Course of Empire.* Boston: Houghton Mifflin, 1952.

———, ed. *The Journals of Lewis and Clark.* Boston: Houghton Mifflin, 1953.

Duncan, Dayton. *Out West: An American Journey.* New York: Viking, 1987.

Fanselow, Julie. *The Traveler's Guide to the Lewis and Clark Trail.* Helena, Mont.: Falcon Press, 1994.

Fischer, Hank, and Carol Fischer. *Paddling Montana.* Helena, Mont.: Falcon Press, 1999.

Flores, Dan L., ed. *Jefferson and Southwestern Exploration: The Freeman and Custis Accounts of the Red River Expedition of 1806.* Norman: University of Oklahoma Press, 1984.

———. *The Natural West: Environmental History in the Great Plains and Rocky Mountains.* Norman: University of Oklahoma Press, 2001.

———. *Southern Counterpart to Lewis and Clark: The Freeman and Custis Expedition of 1806.* Norman: University of Oklahoma Press, 2002.

Furtwangler, Albert. *Acts of Discovery: Visions of America in the Lewis and Clark Journals.* 1993; Urbana: University of Illinois Press, 1999.

Gass, Patrick. *The Journals of Patrick Gass,* edited and annotated by Carol Lynn MacGregor. Missoula. Mont.: Mountain Press, 1997.

Hafen, LeRoy R., ed. *The Mountain Men and the Fur Trade of the Far West.* Glendale, Calif.: Arthur H. Clark, 1965; Lincoln: University of Nebraska Press, 1982.

Harris, Burton. *John Colter: His Years in the Rockies.* New York: Scribner, 1952; Lincoln: University of Nebraska Press, 1993.

Hartley, Robert E. *Lewis and Clark in the Illinois Country: The Little-Told Story.* Westminster, Colo.: Xlibris/Sniktau Publications, 2002.

Holbrook, Stewart. *The Columbia.* New York: Holt, Rinehart & Winston, 1956; San Francisco: Comstock, 1990.

Jackson, Donald, ed. *Letters of the Lewis and Clark Expedition, with Related Documents, 1783–1854.* 2 vols. 2nd ed. Urbana: University of Illinois Press, 1978.

———. *Thomas Jefferson and the Rocky Mountains.* Urbana: University of Illinois Press, 1981; Norman: University of Oklahoma Press, 2002 (page reference is to the 2002 edition).

Josephy, Alvin M. *The Nez Perce Indians and the Opening of the Northwest*. New Haven: Yale University Press, 1965.

Kesselheim, Alan S. *Threading the Currents: A Paddler's Passion for Water*. Washington, D.C.: Island Press, 1998.

Kittredge, William. *Taking Care: Thoughts on Storytelling and Belief*. Minneapolis: Milkweed Editions, 1999.

Krakel, Dean II. *Downriver: A Yellowstone Journey*. San Francisco: Sierra Club Books, 1987.

Large, Arlen J. "Literary Borrowings from Lewis and Clark." *We Proceeded On* vol. 18, no. 2 (May, 1992): 12–19.

———. "The Rocky Boat Ride of Lewis and Clark." *We Proceeded On* vol. 21, no. 1 (February, 1995): 16–23.

Lavender, David. *The Way to the Western Sea: Lewis and Clark across the Continent*. New York: Harper & Row, 1988.

Leopold, Aldo. *A Sand County Almanac*. New York: Oxford University Press, 1949.

Leopold, Luna B. *A View of the River*. Cambridge: Harvard University Press, 1994.

Moulton, Gary. *The Journals of the Lewis and Clark Expedition*. 13 vols. Lincoln: University of Nebraska Press, 1983–2001.

Neihardt, John G. *The River and I*. New York: Putnam, 1910; Lincoln: University of Nebraska Press, 1992.

O'Neil, Paul. *The Rivermen*. New York: Time-Life Books, 1975.

Osgood, Ernest Staples, ed. *The Field Notes of Captain William Clark, 1803–1805*. New Haven: Yale University Press, 1964.

Palmer, Tim. *The Columbia: Sustaining a Modern Resource*. Seattle: The Mountaineers, 1997.

———. *The Snake River*. Washington, D.C.: Island Press, 1991.

Patterson, R. M. *Dangerous River*. New York: William Sloane, 1954; Post Mills, Vt.: Chelsea Green Publishing, 1990.

———. *Far Pastures*. Sydney, British Columbia: Gray's Publishing, 1963; Victoria, British Columbia: Horsdal & Schubert, 1993.

Powell, John Wesley. *The Exploration of the Colorado River and Its Canyons*. Mineola, N.Y.: Dover, 1961.

Ronda, James P. *Finding the West: Explorations with Lewis and Clark*. Albuquerque: University of New Mexico Press, 2001.

———. *Lewis and Clark among the Indians*. 1984; Lincoln: University of Nebraska Press, 2002.

———. *Voyages of Discovery: Essays on the Lewis and Clark Expedition*. Helena: Montana Historical Society Press, 1998.

———, ed. *Thomas Jefferson and the Changing West*. Albuquerque: University of New Mexico Press; St. Louis: Missouri Historical Society Press, 1997.

Saindon, Bob. "The 'Unhappy Affair' on Two Medicine River." *We Proceeded On* vol. 28, no. 3. (August, 2002): 12–25.

———. "The White Pirogue of the Lewis and Clark Expedition. *Proceedings*, Eighth Annual Meeting, Lewis and Clark Trail Heritage Foundation, Inc., August 1976.

Schmidt, Thomas. *The Lewis and Clark Trail*. Washington, D.C.: National Geographic Society, 1998.

Stegner, Wallace. *The Sound of Mountain Waters*. Garden City, N.Y.: Doubleday, 1969.

Snyder, Gerald S. *In the Footsteps of Lewis and Clark*. Washington, D.C.: National Geographic Society, 1970.

Thoreau, Henry David. *Collected Essays and Poems*. New York: The Library of America, 2001.

Udall, Stewart. *The Quiet Crisis*. New York: Holt, Rinehart and Winston, 1963.

Vestal, Stanley. *The Missouri*. New York and Toronto: Farrar & Rinehart, 1945; Lincoln: University of Nebraska Press, 1964.

Western Writers of America, ed., *Water Trails West*. Garden City, N.Y.: Doubleday, 1978.

Wheeler, Olin D. *The Trail of Lewis and Clark, 1804–1806*. 2 vols. New York: G. P. Putnam's Sons, 1904.

Worster, Donald. *Rivers of Empire: Water, Aridity and the Growth of the American West*. New York: Pantheon Books, 1985.

Index

Page numbers for illustrations are indicated by italic type.

ISBN 1-58544-344-1